SACRED SPACES

A Journey with the Sufis of the Indus

Samina Quraeshi

With contributions by
Ali S. Asani ◆ Carl W. Ernst ◆ Kamil Khan Mumtaz

Peabody Museum Press | Mapin Publishing

In the name of God
the Compassionate
the Merciful

CONTENTS

PREFACE

Safar dar watan.
*The real journey must take place within
the wastes of one's homeland, the soul.*

Traditional Sufi saying

My father taught me that all paths lead to God. He spoke of the difference
between religion and faith, of how religion was a matter of interpretation
while faith was ineffable and part of the life of the soul. He believed that
education and tolerance of other points of view were essential companions
on life's journey. My mother, Rahat, stressed that one must conduct one's
life according to the Ten Commandments. As an adult, as the world
continues to confront bigotry and terrorism in the name of Islam, I struggle
to put my own experiences as a Muslim in perspective. It will be a lifelong
quest. This book is a beginning.

A guiding spirit of my work is the late Annemarie Schimmel,
practicing Sufi and eminent scholar of Islam, who was my mentor as I
struggled to understand the spiritual dimensions of my culture of origin
and where I fit into it. I met Dr. Schimmel at Harvard University. She
was Professor of Indo-Muslim Culture, and I was a research scholar at the
Carpenter Center for the Visual Arts. I invited her to visit my studio and
was struck by her insightful observations. She had a keen appreciation for
the symbolism of Islam, and she commented on the influence of my native
Pakistan in my photographs and paintings. Much of my work was inspired
by Islamic theology, but it was also informed by my experience of Islamic
culture as practiced in the specific Indo-Muslim context. My approach
was not rooted in scholarship. But Dr. Schimmel was that rare scholar who

*A prince (Khurram?) and his companions
visit a sage. Unknown artist, mid-seventeenth
century CE.*

ix

encourages exploration of the ineffable. When I attended some of her lectures on the mystical dimensions of Islam she took me aside and said, "Your real work is to express what people feel and cannot express. You must communicate through this talent Allah gave you. Do not waste it. Start."

Dr. Schimmel introduced me to her student Ali Asani, now Professor of Indo-Muslim and Islamic Religion and Cultures at Harvard. Ali was always part of lively discussions on Islam and the events that dominated the news in the 1980s, as Islamic extremists from Iran to Libya began to commandeer the popular Western perception of the Muslim world. Each year, we celebrated Dr. Schimmel's birthday with a feast of her favorite South Asian dishes—*biryani* and chicken *korma*. Amidst the music and conversation of her friends and colleagues many new ideas were born—among them my journey to express in words and images the living traditions of Sufism in the Indus region. As she neared the end of her career, Dr. Schimmel charged Ali with continuing her research path, and she exhorted me to seek his advice when I voiced concerns that, as an artist, I would not be able to express the scholarly dimensions of Sufism.

Ali Asani is deeply interested in the cultural expressions of folk Islam. His discourses on the Ismaili sect and the unique characteristics of the Shi'a and Sunni branches of Islam have aided my own understanding of the nuances of different expressions of faith. Ali graciously carved time from his busy schedule of teaching and writing to advise and support me in the preparation of this book. When I asked him to provide an introduction to the volume, he responded with a lyrical essay that links this journey to the poetic expressions of Sufism in music and verse.

In 2006, I was at the American Academy in Rome researching the Jesuit order and their mission in India at the time of the Mughals. As part of my studies I read *Following Muhammad: Rethinking Islam in the Contemporary World*, by Carl Ernst, a remarkable scholar with great sensitivity to the ethos of Pakistani culture. Annemarie Schimmel had passed away in 2003, and in her absence I was struggling with the many questions about Islam that still confounded me.

When I returned to my studio in Massachusetts, I picked up my copy of Schimmel's *Mystical Dimensions of Islam*. Out of it fell a note in her handwriting. It read: "Samina, you must meet Carl. He is one of my gifted torchbearers and the questions you have are better answered by someone who understands the psyche of your region the way he does." I had already read *Sufi Martyrs of Love*, in which Ernst and Bruce Lawrence explain the Chishtiyya order of Sufis, and I realized that it would take a lifetime to attain the depth of knowledge and understanding shared by these two scholars. I looked up Carl's telephone number in Chapel Hill and called him. It was almost as if he was waiting for my call. He knew who I was, and my incoherent introduction did not discourage him from inviting me to Chapel Hill to talk with him about this project. I found Carl to be enthusiastic about building a bridge between the academy and the public. He offered to contribute to my book his own essay about the mystics of the Indus—their history, their significance to the region, and their place within South Asian Islam. He has been an inspiration and support throughout this endeavor.

In the end, this is a book about sacred places and how the spirit of Sufism is embodied and enacted at the shrines of the saints. The Pakistani architect Kamil Khan Mumtaz has a special understanding of the physical elements of this mystical relationship. Kamil has led me on many tours of his beloved city, Lahore. Each time, he reveals a piece of history that animates the alleys and neighborhoods of the Old City. I realized that the Sufi shrines and *khanqahs* I had visited with my family as a child were a part of our family's ritual observances that I took for granted. I needed to speak with their custodians and with scholars to grasp their significance and ponder their relevance to the present. When I began revisiting the sanctuaries along the Indus, I sought Kamil's advice. At the time, he was designing and constructing a small Sufi shrine at a site in the Old City. Two engineers from England wanted to honor the legacy of Baba Hasan Din, a Sufi shaikh of British birth who was their spiritual guide. They had approached Kamil and asked for his help in building a mausoleum.

While he was designing the mausoleum, Kamil took the two engineers to Lahore's Mughal fort to visit the Pearl Mosque. Kamil decided to ask the custodians if he could go into the lower regions of the fort, which once contained cells for prisoners. He noticed a passageway that was blocked by a latticed screen. Curious, he managed to find a way through the crumbling barrier and found himself in an octagonal chamber with a distinct fragrance of attar of roses. He was surprised and moved to see that the dimensions of this octagonal space were exactly the same as those he had conceived of as the design for his new shrine.

Trained as an architect in the Western tradition, Kamil now works with the spiritual teachings of the Sufis as the inspiration for his architectural designs. He has stories of receiving spontaneous donations when resources are low, of marble carvers appearing when their skills are required. He often wonders if these are coincidence, serendipity, or the fulfillment of pure intentions. Kamil's essay in this volume describes his experience and understanding of sacred spaces as physical places, enhancing our perception of the sanctuaries people have erected over the years to demonstrate the power of their spiritual teacher through the lived experience of a practicing architect.

The contributions of Ali Asani, Carl Ernst, and Kamil Khan Mumtaz provide a background to the individual journey that is the core of this book. The grounding they provide in culture, religion, history, and architecture serves to contextualize my personal narrative and the visual exploration of the sacred spaces of the Indus that have mapped my own spiritual path.

As I have worked on this project I have been consistently reminded of Annemarie's last directions to me. "Samina, you are in the sleep of heedlessness. Do this work and it will lead you; all you need is the intention to use your imagination to awaken your soul."

My journey is a quest to seek the wisdom of the heart, to feel the great spiritual current that flows through all religions, to listen to the telling of sacred narratives that connect history and ritual to each story of seeking. It is my hope that readers can find within my images a message that resonates as they join me in their journey through this book.

Sacred space is unique to each individual: a place where one feels connected to something larger than oneself. It may be in a sanctuary such as the ones I have visited, or some other place where one's connection to faith, history, or experience is especially strong. Sacred spaces have much to teach us about the importance of ritual in our lives and the life of our society. In this work I seek to transcend barriers of language, race, and culture by using the evocative tools of poetry, music, and visual imagery. By exploring a small fraction of the mystical and devotional practices that inflect Indo-Muslim culture, and the spatial patterns that give them form, I offer a humble argument for an artistic method of spiritual investigation: an investigation whose basis is the observation of places and practices, and whose aspiration is the expression of the inexpressible.

Samina Quraeshi

Be in this world
As if you are a stranger or a traveler.

Hadith

الله نورُ السَّمٰوَاتِ وَالْأَرْضِ

ALLAH IS THE LIGHT OF THE HEAVENS AND THE EARTH.

QUR'AN 24:35

Images of South Asian Sufism

Ali S. Asani

> Divine knowledge is revealed to Lovers,
> What do Mullahs and Kazis know about it?
>
> Hear, O Kazi! The refuting argument of Love
> We have love and you have knowledge,
> How can you be reconciled with us?
>
> Sachal Sarmast[1]

South Asia is home to the largest concentration of Muslims in the world. Historically, Sufis and Sufi institutions have played a key role in the transmission of Islamic ideas and practices in the region. Consequently, most South Asian Muslims have traditionally understood their faith through the lens of Sufism. A term that most people commonly associate with spirituality or mysticism, "Sufism" is better understood as a complex cultural phenomenon that is closely intertwined with many aspects of South Asian Muslim societies. We can, therefore, discern its influence extending far beyond devotional practice into the realms of politics and economics. Sufism in South Asia has affected the lives and thought of a wide spectrum of individuals—from emperors and statesmen to philosophers, calligraphers, and musicians.

The most obvious impact of Sufism, however, lies in the realm of popular culture. Sufi poets rank among the pioneers in the use of local languages, popular folk idioms, music, and the inclusion of metaphorical imagery into devotional compositions, thereby influencing the lives of millions of ordinary men and women. As early as the thirteenth century of the Christian era (CE) (the sixth century of the Islamic, or Hijri, calendar [AH]), Sufis began composing short verses for the *sama*, a ritual that involves

Manuscript of a divan of Hafiz.
Unknown artist, c. CE 1540–1550.

the singing of poetry with music and, on occasion, spontaneous dancing. Intended to make listeners and participants forget their material existence and experience spiritual ecstasy by finding God, the *sama* has always attracted large crowds of Muslims and non-Muslims alike to Sufi shrines—the sacred spaces that are the subject of this volume.

I opened this essay with two verses by Sachal Sarmast (d. CE 1826; AH 1241), a prominent early nineteenth-century Sufi poet of Sindh, currently the southern province of Pakistan. Written in the Sindhi language, these verses capture vividly the spirit of Sufism. On one level, the lines express the voices of ordinary people against the religious establishment, challenging the authority of *mullah*s (Muslim religious scholars) and *kazi*s (Muslim religious judges) to interpret Islam on the basis of their learning and scholarship. In these verses Sachal rebukes those who conceive of religion merely in terms of rites and rituals, rules and regulations that must be meticulously followed. But the message that always lies at the core of Sachal's poetry is not rebellion but passionate love of God. As the verses suggest, for Sachal—as for Sufis generally—the surest way to experience and know God is not through knowledge of religious law and theology but by totally immersing oneself in passionate love of the Divine. Like Rabia al-Adawiyya (d. CE 801; AH 184), the woman mystic who ranks among the earliest Sufis to promote the idea of selfless love of God, Sachal was critical of those who worshiped God out of hope of Paradise or out of fear of Hell. Such worship, he felt, was ultimately egotistical for it was self-centered, not God-centered. For him, the only way to worship God was from altruistic love, loving God for God's sake, without any ulterior motive. Viewed from this perspective, *islam,* in its literal sense of "submission," meant submission of the human ego to God out of unconditional love, a love that was passionate and self-consuming. Indeed, Sachal was so overwhelmed by this love that the sobriquet *sarmast,* or "intoxicated one," was attached to his name.

Sachal was one of hundreds of poets in the Indian subcontinent who chose to express key concepts of Sufi Islam in verse form. They composed their poetry in the various vernacular languages understood by the masses rather than in Arabic, Persian, and Sanskrit—cosmopolitan languages that were closely associated with scholarly and religious elites. Their verses were often fused with other aspects of popular culture, and especially with music. For centuries, folk poetry has been an important means of transmitting and disseminating religious ideas in South Asia and singing is a form of worship that continues to characterize popular religious life in the subcontinent. Significantly, the use of this music and verse flourished principally among those Muslim groups who favored a mystical and esoteric interpretation of

سرمد گله اختصار می باید کرد

یک کار ازیں دو کار می باید کرد

یا جان بر رضای دوست می باید داد

یا قطع نظر زیارے می باید کرد

سرمد سرمستؒ

Oh Sarmad, you must stop complaining
You must do one of these two things
Sacrifice your life in service to your beloved
Or sever all contact and turn your eyes from
your beloved.
  Sachal Sarmast

their faith. They enthusiastically embraced poetry and music not only as a means of expression but also as a way of transcending the material and the worldly and experiencing, or "tasting," the spiritual and otherworldly.

The *qawwali*, a genre of Muslim devotional music that is uniquely South Asian in both form and content, is one of the most vibrant expressions of Sufi Islam in the subcontinent today. Deriving its name from the Arabic *qaul,* meaning "spoken word," the *qawwali* is popularly associated with the famous Indo-Persian poet Amir Khusrau (d. CE 1325; AH 725). Tradition holds that Amir Khusrau was encouraged by his Sufi *shaikh,* the eminent Chishti master Nizamuddin Auliya of Delhi, to sing Arabic, Persian, and Hindawi verses in *ragas* based on the musical traditions of northern India. The *qawwali* is usually sung by a group of *qawwals* (singers), who provide the choral support to one or two powerful solo singers by repeating key verses and refrains in rhythms of increasing intensity. The impact of the singing is enhanced by the strong rhythmic patterns of drumming and clapping and is traditionally accompanied by instruments such as the *sarangi* and the *sitar,* which today have been largely replaced by the ubiquitous harmonium. It is believed that when the *zarb,* the pulse or beat of the music and poetry, begins to resonate with the heartbeats of listeners, individual members of the audience will be transported to a state of spiritual ecstasy.

The possibilities for expressing Sufi ideas through poetry and song are seemingly endless. The poet's challenge is to effectively blend a message into the image, to retain its simplicity, and to not weigh it down with burdensome theological speculation. To do so, Sufi poets have always drawn extensively on metaphors and symbols associated with the experience of women—especially their experience of yearning love—to convey their ideas about the soul's relationship to God. In this way they transmit a spiritual and philosophical message that all members of society, the literate as well as the illiterate, can comprehend. Drawing on local literary conventions, Sufi folk poetry always represents the soul as a *virahini,* a loving woman who longs for her absent beloved. The woman-soul becomes, for the folk poet, a standard symbol to express the core message of Sufi thought: the yearning of the human soul for God. In the works of these poets it is easy to discern the influences of songs sung by rural women during periods of separation—those times when they leave their parental homes upon marriage, or when at sunset they anxiously await the return of their husbands from the fields.

The most dramatic use of the woman-soul symbol occurs when Sufi poets interpret folk romances and legends allegorically to express different aspects of the human-divine relationship. Thus, in Hindi-speaking areas, the Radha-Krishna romance from Hindu devotional poetry was furnished with Sufi meaning. Identifying himself with the female Radha, the poet could express the soul's yearning for God. Hindi-speaking Sufi poets, the most prominent of whom were disciples of Chishti masters, composed long and erudite mystic-romantic epics that were modeled after the Persian epics written in the *masnawi* form (narrative verse in rhymed couplets) by poets such as Rumi and Attar. It is the mystical poets writing in Sindhi and Punjabi, however, who refined the technique of reading spiritual meaning into local romances. The heroine in the tales of Heer-Ranjha, Sassi and Punnun (Sassui-Punhun), and Sohni-Mahiwal always searches for her lost beloved until she either finds him or dies trying. She is the seeking soul on the mystical path who, separated from the Divine Beloved, has to undergo great tribulations and a painful purification process in her quest:

> My body burns. With roasting fire
> I am consumed but make my quest.
> Parched am I with the Beloved's thirst
> Yet drinking, find in drink no rest.
> Nay! Did I drain the ocean wide
> 'Twould grant in not one sip a zest.[2]

Poets such as the famous Sindhi mystic Shah Abdul Latif (d. CE 1752; AH 1165), whose shrine is one of the sacred spaces visited here, have ingeniously endowed these heroines with interpretations that resonate with the various Qur'anic verses that Sufis use as proof texts to support their doctrines and practices. Fundamental Sufi ideas concerning the transformation of the *nafs*, the lower self, are effectively presented within this framework. Thus, the heroine Sassi, whose beloved Punnun was kidnapped while she slept, represents the soul in the *khwab-i ghaflat*, "the sleep of negligence," ensnared in the material world and oblivious of the Lord. Marui, the village damsel who, pining for her parental home, spurns the wealth and status offered by her suitor Umar, represents the soul ever yearning for the divine homeland in which it originated. And the foolish queen Lila who, for the sake of a fabulous necklace, "sold" her husband to her maid for a night, represents the *nafs-i ammara*, "the commanding lower-self" (Qur'an 12:53), attracted to the material world and needing to be purified and transformed into the *nafs-i mutmainna*, "the soul at peace" (Qur'an 89:27), before it can be accepted by the Lord.

According to the Sufi saying, "*Safar dar watan*," the real journey must take place within the wastes of one's homeland, the soul. It is only there, according to the Prophet Muhammad's precept of dying to oneself, that one can find the Beloved.

Neither Moses am I, nor Pharaoh
Bulleh who am I, what do I know?
Bulleh Shah

نہ میں موُسے نہ فِرعون

بلّھا کیہ جاناں میں کون؟

بلّھے شاہ

Shah Abdul Latif's Sassi sings of her beloved Punnun:

> As I turned inwards and conversed with my soul
> There was no mountain to surpass and no Punhun to care for.
> I myself became Punhun
> Only while Sassui did I experience grief.[3]

Similarly, his Punjabi contemporary Bulleh Shah (d. CE 1758; AH 1171) has his heroine Heer exclaim of her lost lover Ranjha:

> Repeating Ranjha Ranjha I myself have become Ranjha
> Call me now Dhidho Ranjha, none should call me Heer.[4]

The heroine has become so sublime that her physical quest for the Beloved is transformed into a spiritual one.

The expressive practices and creations of Sufism—its poetry, music, dance, graphic arts, calligraphy, and architecture—continue to have tremendous appeal for the people of contemporary South Asia. In this book, the Pakistani artist Samina Quraeshi offers us a unique account of a journey through her childhood homeland in search of the wisdom of the Sufis. Along this meandering path she has created an imaginative personal history and a rich body of photographs and works of art, all of which reflect the seeking heart of the Sufi Way. Her colleagues Carl Ernst and Kamil Khan Mumtaz provide signposts on the journey. In the aftermath of 9/11, Sufi practices and the creative work they inspire present a refreshingly different face of Islam, speaking in a voice that directly challenges the intolerance of politically motivated groups such as the Taliban. The work presented in this volume builds on the centuries-old Sufi tradition of mystical messages of love, freedom, and tolerance that continue to offer the promise of building cultural and spiritual bridges between peoples of different faiths living in South Asia and around the world.

NOTES

1. Advani, *Sachal,* 30–31.
2. Sorley, *Shah Abdul Latif of Bhit,* 255.
3. Jotwani, *Shah Abdul Latif,* 136.
4. Rama Krishna, *Punjabi Sufi Poets,* 63.

الصُّوفي إذا انطَق بأن نُطقَه مِن الحقائق وإن سكَت نَطقَت
عَنهُ الجَوارِحُ بقَطع العَلَاقَت   قول ذوالنون مصري

WHEN THE SUFI SPEAKS IT IS THE TRUTH.
WHEN THE SUFI IS SILENT HE IS REFLECTING ON THE TRUTH.

QAUL ZAWA AL NOON MISRI

Islam and Sufism in Contemporary South Asia

Carl W. Ernst

The South Asian subcontinent—comprising India, Pakistan, Bangladesh, Afghanistan, and neighboring countries—is home to one-third of the world's Muslims today. What mostly passes for information about this region in the news media is focused on conflict in its many modes: communal clashes, terrorism, and war. Missing from these sensationalist portrayals are all the elements of local culture that give life its flavor. For the majority of the hundreds of millions of South Asian Muslims, life is not defined by the frightened concerns of journalism. If we wish to have a better view of the distinctive factors that might constitute South Asian Islam, we will have to look elsewhere than in the bastions of Islamic fundamentalism. The rhythms of local culture cluster around sacred shrines, tombs of the great Sufi saints that punctuate the landscapes of both rural outposts and downtown streets. These places of holiness, many of which are architectural jewels, are arguably some of the most important centers of South Asian Islam.

There are, of course, other ways in which one may approach the geographic specification of an Islamic culture in the South Asian subcontinent. Bruce Lawrence has demonstrated two such approaches in a pair of brilliant though conceptually very different articles written for encyclopedias. In one of these, "Islam in South Asia," he adopts a peripheral approach and looks at the most far-flung regions of the subcontinent (including Bengal and Kerala) to provide an off-centered perspective.[1] In the other, "The Eastward Journey of Muslim Kingship," he presents a vivid narrative of the imperial institutions of the Mughals as a lens through which to view the formation of Muslim society.[2] Another and much more extensive cultural treatment was Annemarie Schimmel's volume on *Islam in*

Two dervishes; folio from an album. Unknown artist, c. CE 1910–1920.

21

the Indian Subcontinent, which is indeed a classic in its comprehensiveness and its remarkable command of the sources.[3]

The approach under consideration here is different from Lawrence's scholarly articles and more complementary to the cultural perspective of Annemarie Schimmel. It is the result of the personal journey of one South Asian Muslim woman, Samina Quraeshi. A personal perspective such as hers is admittedly subjective and centered on particular sets of experiences. Quraeshi speaks to the deep spiritual appeal of the major centers of Sufism in the central and northwestern heartlands of South Asia. She invokes the rural landscapes of the Punjab and the Gangetic plain, as well as the ancient cities of Lahore and Delhi. Although her vision does not by any means exhaust the astonishing complexities of the culture of South Asian Muslims, it does bring into play traditions of great importance for the understanding of South Asian Islam.

The sense of a distinctive destiny for South Asian Islam is not new. As early as the thirteenth century, the historian Minhaj-i Siraj saw Muslim India as the bulwark of Islam, and indeed its central redoubt, in the aftermath of the catastrophe of the Mongol invasion of the Middle East and the overthrow of the caliphate in CE 1258 (AH 655). Muslim rulers not only in the Delhi sultanate but also in outlying kingdoms maintained the symbolism of the caliphate in their own coinage for over a century after this blow to notions of Islamic sovereignty. The persistence of the imperial idea of the caliphate in such a fictional mode, as Toynbee would have put it, was at the same time a powerful assertion by Indo-Muslim rulers of their role in preserving that Islamic legacy. Certain rulers shored up the Turkish–Central Asian concept of world-imperial rule with patronage of Islamic law, as in the case of Sultan Firuz Shah ibn Tughluq; in the late fourteenth century he proclaimed his renunciation of non-*sharia* instruments of government and methods of taxation, while at the same time he commissioned numerous scholarly works on the teachings of Islamic law. By associating his regime with the authority of Islamic law and texts containing legal rulings, he argued that his imperial legitimacy derived from religion rather than from the raw power of royal authority; paradoxically, it was only that royal authority that permitted him to claim Islamic legitimacy. In a similar fashion, the Mughal emperor Aurangzeb (d. CE 1707; AH 1118) appealed to Islamic symbols and institutions in his sponsorship of collections of legal responsa (the famous *Fatawa-i Alamgiri*) and by introducing Islamic touches to the edifice of Mongol and Persian monarchy constructed by his forebears Akbar, Jahangir, and Shah Jahan.

Yet as Samina Quraeshi makes clear, the institute of kingship cannot be seen as the real locus of the culture of South Asian Muslims, despite the

23

romantic fascination of its tales of courtly intrigue and power. To get to the heart of India's role in the Muslim cosmos one has to go back considerably further. This powerful insight was deployed at length in a late Arabic masterwork of the Indian poet and scholar Ghulam Ali Azad Bilgrami (d. CE 1786; AH 1200), who pointed out in his *Coral Rosary of Indian Traditions* that India plays a central role in the most canonical of Islamic sources, the sayings of the Prophet Muhammad, known collectively as *hadith*. As abundantly illustrated, for instance, in the massive *History of the Prophets and Kings* by al-Tabari (d. CE 923; AH 310), India was the site of one of the primordial dramas in the cosmology of Islam: the descent of Adam from paradise to earth.[4] It was on a mountaintop in the great island of Sarandib, as the Arabs called it—Ceylon, or modern Sri Lanka—that Adam first set foot on earth; the spot today is known appropriately as Adam's Peak, though the massive footprint enshrined there is also revered as Buddha's or Shiva's by devotees from Buddhist and Hindu backgrounds. But for Muslims, it has been a sacred spot for centuries. Consider the report of the famous traveler Ibn Battuta in the early fourteenth century:

> The mountain of Sarandib is one of the highest in the world. We saw it from the sea when we were nine days' journey away, and when we climbed it we saw the clouds below us, shutting out our view of its base. On it there are many evergreen trees and flowers of various colours, including a red rose as big as the palm of a hand. There are two tracks on the mountain leading to the Foot, one called Baba track and the other Mama track, meaning Adam and Eve. The Mama track is easy and is the route by which the pilgrims return, but anyone who goes by that way is not considered by them to have made the pilgrimage at all. The Baba track is difficult and stiff climbing. Former generations cut a sort of stairway on the mountain, and fixed iron stanchions on it, to which they attached chains for climbers to hold on by. There are ten such chains, two at the foot of the hill by the "threshold," seven successive chains farther on, and the tenth is the "Chain of the Profession of Faith," so-called because when one reaches it and looks down to the foot of the hill, he is seized by apprehensions and recites the profession of faith ("There is no god but God, and Mohammed is His messenger!") for fear of falling. When you climb past this chain you find a rough track. From the tenth chain to the grotto of Khidr is seven miles; this grotto lies in a wide plateau, and nearby it is a spring full of fish, but no one catches them. Close to this there are two tanks cut in the rock on either side of the path. At the grotto of Khidr the pilgrims leave their belongings and ascend thence for two miles to the summit of the mountain where the Foot is.

The blessed Footprint, the Foot of our father Adam, is on a lofty black rock in a wide plateau. The blessed Foot sank into the rock far enough to leave its impression hollowed out. It is eleven spans long. In ancient days the Chinese came here and cut out of the rock the mark of the great toe and the adjoining parts. They put this in a temple at Zaytun, where it is visited by men from the farthest parts of the land. In the rock where the Foot is there are nine holes cut out, in which the infidel pilgrims place offerings of gold, precious stones, and jewels. You can see the dervishes, after they reach the grotto of Khidr, racing one another to take what there is in these holes. We, for our part, found nothing in them but a few stones and a little gold, which we gave to the guide. It is customary for the pilgrims to stay at the grotto of Khidr for three days, visiting the Foot every morning and evening, and we followed this practice. When the three days were over we returned to the Mama track, halting at a number of villages on the mountain. At the foot of the mountain there is an ancient tree whose leaves never fall, situated in a place that cannot be got at. I have never met anyone who has seen its leaves.[5]

I cite this report at length so one can get the flavor of the experience of this Muslim judge from Morocco as he approached the shrine of Adam's foot. The atmosphere is rich in mythical overtones, with gendered approaches for pilgrims and a liminal grotto dedicated to the immortal prophet Khizr, which still attracts dervishes and other devotees today.[6] Four centuries later, Azad Bilgrami commented on the popularity of the site, its Sufi attendants, and the friendly "Hindu" ruler (actually a Theravada Buddhist) who welcomed Muslim visitors. More importantly, for Azad, India was, next to Mecca and Medina, the holiest spot in the world for Muslims: it was the site of the first *hajj,* or pilgrimage to the holy city of Mecca (since Adam left India seeking Eve, who had landed in the Arabian town of Jedda), it was the place where all arts, sciences, and rarities had been first revealed on earth, and the locus of the first manifestation of Muhammad's spiritual reality through Adam. In short, concluded Bilgrami, since we are all children of Adam, we are all in fact Indians.

And even in the realm of the formal traditions of Arabic-Islamic scholarship, Bilgrami maintained that it had been primarily the non-Arabs—Persians, Turks, and of course Indians—who had done the most to advance the arts and sciences, particularly through the medium of the Arabic language. While he acknowledged that the Muslims of India had focused their attention primarily on the lives of the Sufi saints, for whom they held such affection (we shall return to this momentarily), he provided

25

his own account of biographies of Islamic scholars nourished in al-Hind (as the Arabs called the subcontinent). What is most interesting about this eighteenth-century portrait, written shortly before the successful onslaught of British colonial rule, is the breadth of intellectual perspective reflected in the lives of South Asian Muslim scholars. While Qur'anic studies and particularly Prophetic *hadith* among the Islamic religious sciences were favored by the Indians, these scholars had strong linkages to the Sufi orders, and many were seriously engaged with philosophical traditions going back to the ancient Greeks. Moreover, they were deeply immersed in the humanistic tradition of Arabic and Persian poetry. Further, Bilgrami himself demonstrated a thorough mastery of Indian literary traditions, which he described in the latter parts of the *Coral Rosary* by providing extensive specimens of Arabic poetry to demonstrate the figures of Indian rhetoric and the different types of lovers. The cosmopolitanism and civility exemplified by Bilgrami were undoubtedly sustained, both intellectually and materially, by the networks of Indian Sufi centers that were constructed around the tombs of the saints.[7]

So in what way can it be said that the Sufi saints provide a defining influence for South Asian Islam? One might take as an emblem of this phenomenon a song made famous in the repertoire of the celebrated *qawwali* singer, the late Nusrat Fateh Ali Khan, which celebrates the lineage of the great Chishti saints of the thirteenth and fourteenth centuries. With powerful rhythm and emphasis, the refrain is enunciated: "God, Muhammad, the Four Friends (*Allah Muhammad chahar yar*): Hajji, Khwaja, Qutb, Farid." This is a clear reference to Hajji Uthman Harwani (d. CE 1211; AH 607), Khwaja Muinuddin Chishti (d. CE 1236; AH 633), Qutbuddin Bakhtiyar Kaki (d. CE 1235; AH 632), and Fariduddin Ganj-i Shakar (d. CE 1265; AH 663). Their very names encapsulate a sacred geography. Uthman Harwani was the last Chishti master to reside in the Afghan town of Chisht, while his successors oversaw the transfer of the order to India; Muinuddin's tomb is in Ajmer in Rajasthan, Qutbuddin's tomb is in the south of Delhi, while Fariduddin's shrine lies in Pakpattan in the Pakistani Punjab. These sacred centers still attract multitudes today, with visitors ranging from elite Sufi disciples to ordinary people from all walks of life.

To give but one example of an elite seeker of solace from these saints, one may consider Jahanara, the Mughal princess, daughter of Shah Jahan and sister to both Dara Shikoh and Aurangzeb. She used her scholarly bent to author biographies of her mentor, the Qadiri shaikh Mullah Shah, and of Muinuddin Chishti as well. Her modest tomb is in the precincts of the shrine of Farid al-Din's successor, Shaikh Nizamuddin Auliya (d. CE 1325; AH 725), in Delhi, where her plain tombstone reads: "Let no one cover my

Verses about a father sending his son on the Sufi Path; folio from an album. Unknown artist and date.

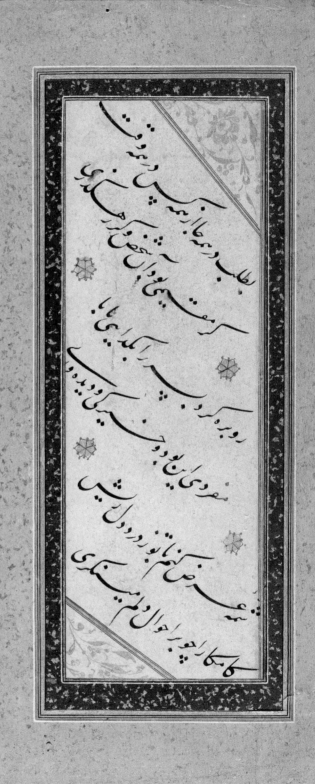

shrine with anything but greenery, for grass is enough as the grave-cover for the poor." Countless ordinary folk also attend the shrines of the saints, particularly at the festival of the death anniversary (*urs*), when benefits both spiritual and material may be sought. The intercession of the saints for divine favor has, however, been challenged in modern times by those who favor the austere approach of Salafi or Wahhabi reformism.

It is remarkable to consider the extent to which the Sufi saints have elicited passionate and loyal followings among non-Muslims. The classic case is probably the aforementioned Fariduddin Ganj-i Shakar, one of the key figures in the Chishti Sufi lineage. While he was thoroughly educated in the scholarly languages of Arabic and Persian, his mother tongue was evidently an early form of Punjabi (only described as Hindawi or "Indian language" in the Persian texts). He and other Sufis born in India habitually composed poetry in their native dialects, although in his case these occasional verses attained immortality when they became enshrined in the sacred scripture of the Sikhs, the Guru Granth Sahib. Despite the skepticism of colonial British scholars like MacAuliffe, the authenticity of the Farid verses in the Guru Granth Sahib seems to be confirmed by manuscript evidence in fourteenth-century Chishti writings from the Deccan.[8] In the realm of religious practice, the presence of Hindus, Sikhs, Christians, and others at major Sufi shrines is a well-attested social phenomenon that shows no sign of disappearing, despite the criticism of purists on all sides. Just to cite one example, the tomb of Shahul Hamid, a famous sixteenth-century saint of South India, was constructed in his honor by the Hindu king Maharaja Pratap Singh (there is also a smaller version of it on the Malaysian island of Penang, built by Indian immigrants). There are numerous places in the South Asian subcontinent (like the shrine of Adam's Peak) where the presence of Sufi saints affords multiple clienteles the possibility of constructing their own relationships with sainthood.

Any visit to a major Sufi shrine in South Asia in fact provides significant evidence that the nominal rulers of the region (kings and sultans) tacitly acknowledged the superior status of saintly authority. Many of the chief Sufi shrines were constructed by rulers such as Shah Jahan, who sought from their benefactions for the saints a spiritual virtue that their own personal actions could not achieve. More poignantly, on the outskirts of many a vibrant Sufi shrine, whitewashed or sometimes colorfully painted, one sees the drab abandoned tombs of kings who hoped that proximity to the saints would compensate for the crimes they committed. Thus throughout premodern South Asia, the Sufi saints were considered to be the real kings, the ones to whom God had entrusted authority over the world.

But the role of the Sufi saints as intermediaries and arbiters of human destiny has been seriously challenged in recent years, most notably by those textually based movements that seek doctrinal purity and religious authenticity in a return to the imagined origins of their religion. Thus pilgrimage to Sufi shrines has been denounced by modern Muslim reformists as idolatry and condemned as the probable result of trafficking with polytheistic Hindus. This kind of fundamentalism is of course found not only among Muslims but also in Hindu circles. It is important to recognize the comparative novelty of these movements, despite their appeal to ancient authority. The advent of British colonialism and the demise of native elites spelled the demise of the institutions of higher education that had fostered the cosmopolitanism documented by Azad Bilgrami. After the abortive 1857 Indian revolt against the British, new forms of Muslim piety arose, like the Deoband academy, which focused its curriculum on the *hadith*, sayings of the Prophet Muhammad, as the source for judgments on every imaginable question of behavior and religious teaching. What was new in Deoband was in a sense modern and technical: print technology replacing the manuscript for dissemination of knowledge, in a bureaucratic educational regime modeled on British precedents. It was also a retrenchment that focused on sacred texts to the exclusion of all else, though couched in a modern medium. Yet it was, in the end, an explicit rejection of the culture of the British overlords—at the cost of much that was local and cultural in origin.

In recent years, it has become fashionable to portray the *madrasah* academies as one-dimensional sources of fanaticism. Much of this perception is based on the role of Deoband-related schools located in refugee camps on Pakistan's North West Frontier province, which played a mobilizing role in organizing *jihad* in collaboration with the Taliban. Breathless journalists continue to file reports on these academic centers as the sources of anti-Americanism, wishfully seeking to isolate what is seen as the irrational source of violent activity. In reality the situation is much more complex. It is still possible for Deoband theologians to be well versed in their Rajput genealogies according to the great Hindu epic, the Mahabharata.[9] And as a recent author has indicated, the experience of going through these *madrasahs* can vary quite dramatically from one institution to another.[10] So it is important to note that many Deoband scholars retain their connections to the Sufi orders, especially since the founders of Deoband were disciples of the Chishti master Hajji Imdad Allah.

Perhaps the most important and decisive variable for the Indian subcontinent has been the factor of nationalism. Often couched in terms that meld religion with ethnic or linguistic identity, this has become such

a potent force that it often threatens to overwhelm everything else in its path. The Partition of British India in 1947 into India and Pakistan along roughly religious lines had devastating effects on the populations subjected to territorial transfer, including the deaths of as many as two million people. Its sequel was the similarly catastrophic breakup of Pakistan in the 1971 Bangladesh war of independence, whose tale of tragic violence has never been fully told. The Islamic Republic of Pakistan has been subject to numerous contradictions in the attempt to enunciate its identity as either a land for Muslims or alternatively as an Islamic state.

The tensions of this paradox were made clear to me one evening at a typical dinner party in Islamabad, when a senior Pakistani diplomat confided to me a parable in which he compared the birth of Pakistan and its sense of identity to the ritual recitation of the call to prayer (*azan*) to a newborn infant. Pakistan at its birth, he told me, heard two *azans* recited into its ears. One of these *azans* was secular and nationalist. It said, "You are a nation, you have geographic boundaries, a history based on the land, with languages and a culture that are your very own, and you must defend them." The other *azan* was religious. It said, "You are a Muslim, your religion is Islam, and it is your destiny to follow the divine will by implementing that religious vision."

Was Pakistan to be a state to safeguard the interests of Muslims, or was it to be an Islamic state? Both of these *azans* spoke to the inner character of Pakistan, but there has always been a gap between them, which the Pakistan of history has never been able to bridge. The parable deftly encapsulates the dilemma faced by Pakistanis attempting to define their national identity. Are they a distinctive nation with their own local traditions based on culture, history, and ethnicity? Or is their identity essentially religious, predicated upon timeless principles derived from sacred scripture, transcending history and locality? Both perspectives have their ardent supporters, and it is the negotiation between them that determines the ongoing political discourse of Pakistan today. But the most disastrous recent influence on the region has been the corrosive effects of weapons, money, and drugs unleashed by decades of the Afghan war, and then the *jihadi* irregulars formerly sponsored by the CIA. Now, proponents of Islamic ideology have been ceded considerable political leverage by a succession of military governments and weak elected rulers who lacked political legitimacy. As a result, merely uttering the word "Islam" is enough to bring conversation to a halt. And ideologues have not failed to take advantage of the power that their claim to represent Islam confers.

The rise of monolithic interpretations of Islam is ironic, however, because Islam has never meant one thing, nor will it in the future.

History reveals multiple interpretive authorities clustered around core texts and practices, with variations manifest in local traditions. That is to say, there are many different commentators who claim to know how to interpret Islam in an authoritative way. Some are legalists, others are mystics representing local lineages, and yet others have proposed new understandings based on new psychological or scientific theories of European origin, or purely idiosyncratic interpretations. There is no Muslim Pope who is the single authority; instead, a cheerful anarchy of a thousand flowers blooms. Modern communications, together with the new concept of Islam as an anticolonial ideology, have made it appealing to invoke the idea of Muslim unity, unrealistic though that may be. Dissident views are discouraged as fractures in the idealized universal community of Muslims. Distinctive local practices are frowned upon as deviations from a homogeneous norm. Yet who is entitled to decide what Islam is, once and for all?

At the same time that globalizing communications have opened up the possibility of a monolithic Islamist discourse, previously unheard voices are now being heard. Among the new developments is a re-evaluation of tradition by feminists, including Islamist women. While it will be tempting for development-minded Euro-American feminists to view their own trajectory as the only possible model for Muslim women, they will need to resist that assumption if they wish to hear the actual voices of their Muslim sisters. We are likewise now able to hear the voices of Muslim minority groups, including those who have been dismissed as sectarian heretics. Countries like Pakistan that define themselves as Islamic states are wrestling

with the questions of the rights of women and the rights of religious minorities as human rights issues. These debates about pluralism will answer not only to local constituencies but also to international scrutiny through the media.

Who has the authority to define Islam? The pragmatic pluralism of historical times and places works against the will to power that would reduce Islam to a single voice. One can listen to the voice of Samina Quraeshi, who proposes instead a multiple, locally inflected vision of Islam in South Asia that is enriched by art and that takes account of both feminine and masculine perspectives. The poverty of recent ideology can be overcome by tapping the richness of an imagination based on the historical depth of culture. It is in this sense that I hope readers will benefit from the perspectives that this book presents on the Sufi tradition that is a key feature of the complex Islamic culture of South Asia today.

Notes

1. Lawrence, "Islam in South Asia."
2. Lawrence, "The Eastward Journey of Muslim Kingship."
3. Schimmel, *Islam in the Indian Subcontinent*.
4. Ernst, "India as a Sacred Islamic Land."
5. Ibn Battuta, *Travels in Asia and Africa*, 258–259.
6. See the rich textual and visual documentation of the Khizr shrine near Adam's Peak (and its parallel Hindu and Buddhist interpretations), available online at the Kathirkamam web site: http://kataragama.org/islamic.htm.

7. For further details on Bilgrami's work, see my article, "Indian Islam: Reconfiguration of the Relation between Religion and World in Sufism and Reformist Islam since the 18th Century," presented at the conference on "Religion and Civil Society—Germany, Great Britain and India in the 19th Century" at WZB Berlin on 10–13 May 2006.

8. Ernst, *Eternal Garden*, 166–168.

9. Shail Mayaram, "Rethinking Meo Identity: Cultural Faultline, Syncretism, Hybridity or Liminality?," *Comparative Studies of South Asia, Africa and the Middle East* 17 (1997), 35–44, http://www.cssaame.ilstu.edu/issues/V17%2D2/MEO.pdf.

10. Ebrahim Moosa, "Inside the Madrasa: A Personal History," *Boston Review* 32.1 (2007), http://bostonreview.net/BR32.1/moosa.html.

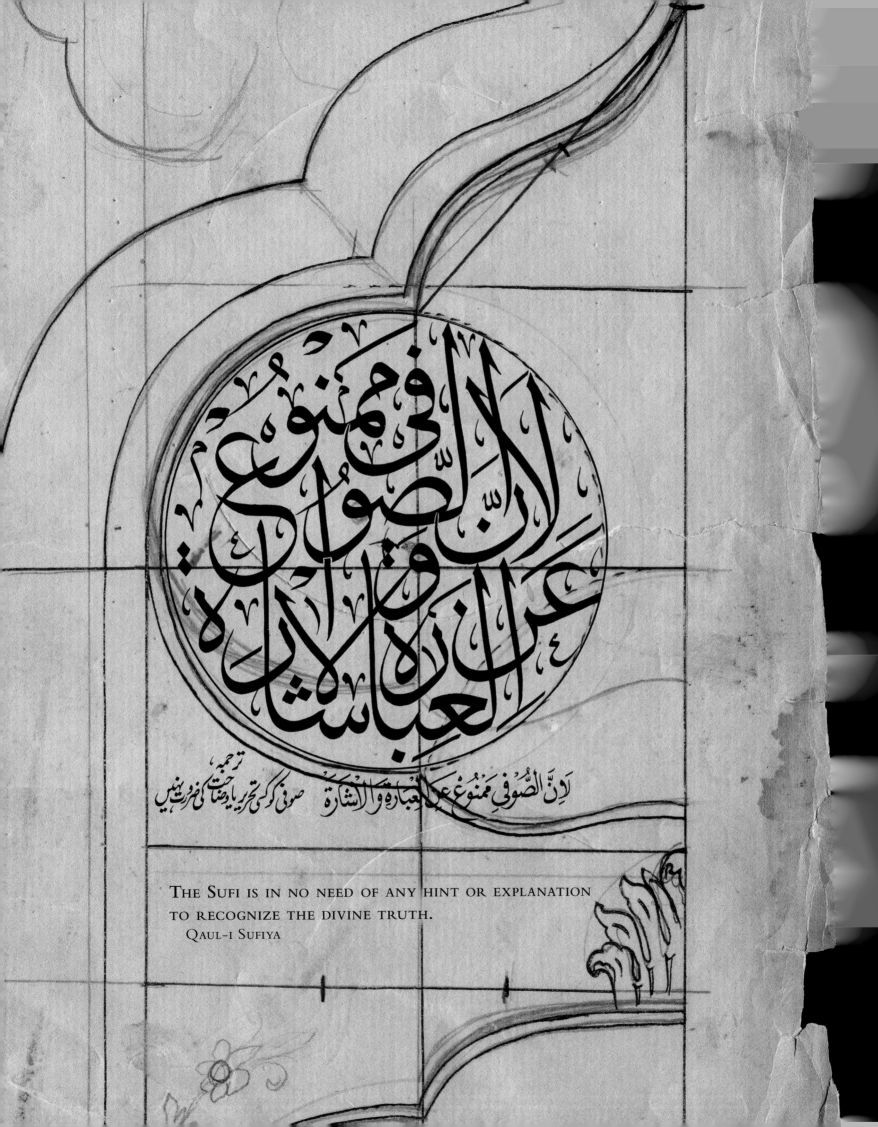

لاِنَّ الصُوفِي مَمْنُوع عَنِ العِبَارَةِ وَالاِشَارَةِ   صوفی کو کسی تحریر یا وضاحت کی ضرورت نہیں

THE SUFI IS IN NO NEED OF ANY HINT OR EXPLANATION
TO RECOGNIZE THE DIVINE TRUTH.
QAUL-I SUFIYA

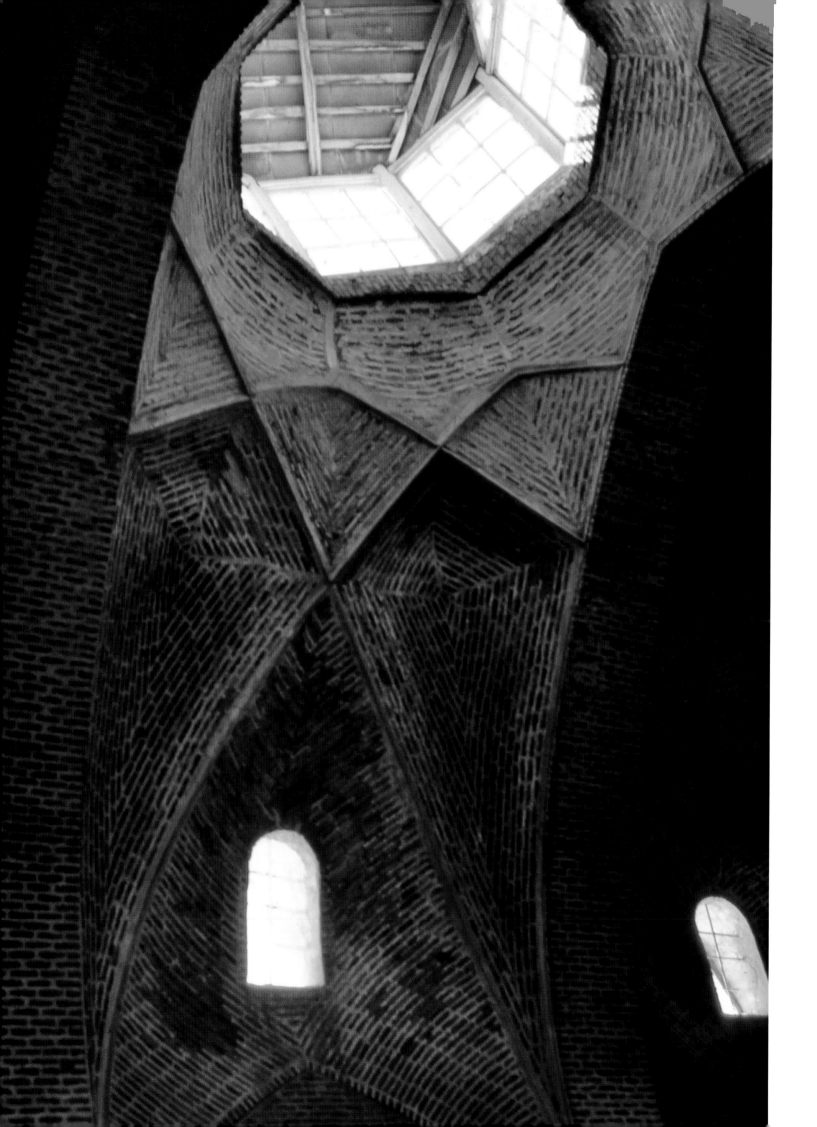

THE ARCHITECTURE OF SUFI SHRINES

Kamil Khan Mumtaz

Sacredness is an attribute we associate with the Divine, and sacred spaces are those that make us aware of the presence of the Divine. This may be due to the natural quality of the space or it may result from the association of the place with, or presence of, holy relics, pious persons, or the performance of religious rites. Temples, churches, and mosques may be considered sacred as symbols representing the "house" of a deity or a "heavenly city" or as physical places of worship. Other structures may be built to demarcate or enclose a sacred space or holy relic, or, as in the case of the Sufi shrine, they may be constructed over the earthly remains of a saint.

Historians may study the architecture of Sufi shrines to trace the evolution of their styles, architects to analyze their form in terms of function, space, and light, and engineers to describe their structure and materials. But to understand the meaning and intentions of the builders and users of these shrines, we need to listen to their authentic voices; we need to turn to the reliable internal evidence provided by inscriptions on the monuments themselves and by other documented sources.

We are fortunate to have the account of the design and construction of the tomb of a Sufi saint by a sixteenth-century Lahore architect, Ustad Bazid, "that rare and wondrous visionary, that fashioner of images, that unraveler of mysteries, and that engineer of the workshop of God's industry who came to be known by the title of Founder of the Second Ka'ba and who was without parallel in the science of architecture and unique in piety and worship."[1] He tells us that he was the son of "an ordinary mason who worked with mud mortar":

In my childhood [my father] would take me by the hand and would show me the tall and grand buildings. My interest increased day by day and the window of my understanding opened extraordinarily. While I was still a youth without a beard my model making and artistic skills became exemplars for experienced gentlemen. A few months after the demise of the exalted Sheikh, my eternal good fortune stirred in me a desire and in the company of some of my young colleagues, I arrived as a pilgrim at the radiant grave at Shergarh [some 80 km south of Lahore].

I saw that stacks of bricks were being collected. So I requested the keeper of the public kitchen, Sheikh Musa, to give me permission for whatever was being planned to be constructed. "What we require," he replied, "is that some elderly professional should prepare a model and then lay the bricks." On hearing this we became saddened and returned to Lahore. After my return the curator was honoured by a visitation from the exalted Sheikh in a dream. His Eminence declared that the work of this construction is to be entrusted to that young man who was turned away. Thereupon the keeper sent two servants after me. Anyhow, I was called back from Lahore and entrusted the work as ordered by His Eminence. When the work commenced experts from every direction got together. I was a novice, and much perturbed I fell to thinking about how the model would take shape. I spent endless nights working with pen and paper. But finally got the work started. Before every brick that we put in place I would invoke God's blessings upon the holy Prophet, may Allah's blessings and peace be upon him. Virtuous men, devotees and seekers of the spiritual path would recite the chapter *Ikhlas* [Qur'an 112] twice over as they passed on each load of bricks or mortar. There were so many people and such a crowd that each turn to hand over the bricks would take rather a long while and with great difficulty. In this manner the construction of the radiant tomb was accomplished in four years. The following chronogram [an inscription in which

certain letters, read as numerals, stand for a particular date], was written on its completion:

> This pure tomb of Hazrat Dawood
> May God forever spread its shadow wide
> By the radiant beauty of its appearance
> The eyes gain sight of the light of God
> He who looks upon it with the eye of meditation
> Can not take his gaze away from it
> To the chant of "*La ilaha illah hoo*" (there is no God but He)
> When recited beneath this dome
> From this which has no parallel
> comes forth the sound of "*wahdahoo la shareek*" (He is one and has no associate)
> To determine the year of its completion
> it has been said "*muddi zillahoo abda*" (extend its shadow to eternity)

Thus we see that the tomb is conceived and built as an act of devotion by pious souls. It embodies the spiritual presence, the *hazrat*, of a saint, and the intention or purpose of its construction is to "spread its shadow wide"; that is, to propagate the guidance and teachings of the saint. We are told that the "radiant beauty of its appearance" is designed to enable the seeker to "gain sight of the light of God." For the adept on the Sufi Path, "who looks upon it with the eye of meditation," it is a support, a vehicle that brings him into communion with the Divine.

The intimate relation of the architecture of the Sufi shrine to Islamic spirituality illustrates the profound connection between the traditional arts and crafts and the metaphysical and idealist worldview common to all traditional societies. Two essential components of the traditional design method, building practices, and design theories that have formed the basis of traditional Islamic architecture are proportioning and the use of "ideal forms." The use of proportional subdivision as a method for determining the size and shape of buildings, rather than relying on a fixed measure

such as a foot or a yard, is well documented. But proportions alone do not determine the form of a building. All spatial relationships are proportionate, and several systems of proportions have been used for buildings of the same type, category, or genre. Indeed, the proportions of a particular building may apply equally to a man, an animal, or a tree. Proportions apply to specific forms and every traditional building type has a predetermined essential typology: a prototype or "ideal" form. Needless to say, however, no two buildings of the same type are in fact identical. A single ideal form may be manifested in an infinite variety of scales, proportions, and details of construction and decorations while "being" essentially a *mandala, yantra,* or *hasht bihisht.*[2] This diversity is due to the specific materials, topology of the site, user requirements, climate, and other conditions. Nevertheless, the work of the designer begins with copying from a preexisting model.

To understand the importance of copying, both as a method of design and as a method of instruction, it is necessary to understand the central place of ideal forms in both the traditional Islamic theory of aesthetics and the creative process within a traditional cosmology that is centered on the relationship between Man, Being, and Manifestation. This relationship is best illustrated by the *hadith qudsi,* a related oral tradition in which God speaks on the tongue of the Prophet: *Kunto kanzan makhfiyyan fa-ahbabto an u'rifa fa-khalaqtul khalq le-u'rifa:* "I was a Hidden Treasure [nonmanifest, Absolute Being, or All Possibility] and I loved to be known [to be manifest], and so I created the world [the physical, material cosmos] that I might be known." In other words, the purpose of the creation of the cosmos is to manifest the qualities, the attributes, of the Creator.

The Qur'anic account of the creation of Man tells us that God made his body of clay, then blew into him of His own Spirit and taught him the names of every thing. Man is thus both earthly body and Divine Spirit: He has both a lower animal self and a higher angelic Self. And while everything in the created universe manifests or reflects some quality of the Creator, only Man "knows" the names of every thing. That is, only Man, potentially, knows the cosmos and manifests or reflects all of the qualities of God, who is none other than the higher Self.

44

In this construct, the macrocosm comprises a hierarchy of layers that can be broadly grouped into three worlds, planes, or dimensions: the earthly world of matter, bound by space and time (this is the earthly world of quantity); above this is the intermediate world of the heavens, the "imaginal"[3] plane (the world of forms); and above these is the "ideal" plane, the spiritual or angelic world (the world of the archetypes, of the essences or qualities, and of pure Being). These three levels correspond in the human microcosm to the body, the soul, and the spirit.

In its broad sense, the term "art" includes all the arts and crafts and is applied to making or doing anything that meets the dual criteria of utility and beauty. Utility—appropriateness to function and purpose—relates to *quantity* and the more obvious practical and physical aspects of material and form. But beauty relates to *quality* and is understood as an aspect of the Divine. In the creative process, the attributes and qualities of the Divine are reflected first as archetypes on the ideal plane of the Spirit, then as pure forms on the imaginal plane, and finally as natural and man-made objects and acts on the earthly plane. Some objects and acts are more "transparent" than others, meaning that the ideal forms are more readily recognized in them than in those that are more "opaque." Qualities such as proportion, harmony, balance, and symmetry, for example, are most readily recognized in certain mathematical relationships, in music, and in other works of art. Similarly, a human form—or a tree or a sunset—may strike us as "perfect" because it corresponds with our idea of a "perfect" human, or tree, or sunset. In this system every earthly object, artifice, or act takes on symbolic meaning to the extent that it reflects its heavenly archetype.[4]

The fully realized or "perfected man," *insan e kamil*, is a mirror that reflects all of the qualities of absolute Being. This is his essential nature, his true self, and the potential exists within every human. But we are veiled from the knowledge of the Real by the phenomenal world, and we are veiled from our true Self by our animal desires. To realize his potential man must recover his primordial nature, made in the image of God but lost at the Fall. It is when his human nature recovers its original wholeness that access to the Spirit, the "eye of the heart," becomes possible. He must undertake an inward journey from the body, through the soul to the heart, the seat of the Spirit. Only when the eye of the heart is opened can it contemplate the Real and gain enlightenment, or "sight of the light of God."[5]

The role of art in traditional Islamic societies has been to act as support in man's spiritual quest or journey toward enlightenment by reminding us of our role and function in this life, by pointing to our true goal, and by illuminating the way to that goal. Within this framework the artist or craftsman cannot presume to be "original" (except in the sense of returning to the origin) or to "create" beauty. Beauty already exists, as an objective reality, and the artist can only aspire to reflect it in his work. But how can he reflect a heavenly archetype that by definition lies beyond this sensible world, the phenomenal world of matter, space, and time?

To begin with, every artist or craftsman acquires his skill from a recognized master. The master, in turn, invariably traces the source of his art through a chain of masters to a divinely inspired source—a prophet, a saint, a sage, or a great master who was both skilled in his art and spiritually enlightened. But none of these sources claim to be the originators or creators of the art in question, only to have been the vehicles or recipients of these gifts from the Divine Spirit. This is why the great classical forms in traditional art and craft—handed down from master to apprentice, from generation to generation—are held in such veneration and esteem. They are copied by students not only as a means of perfecting their technical skills, but also as a means of purifying the spirit or acquiring a special blessing. They are used by professionals as exemplars and points of reference, a guiding framework for their work.

The ideal forms, in themselves, as well as their components and embellishments, can be read as a language of symbols whose meanings may be implicit, as in architectonic elements, in geometric patterns, and floral or other natural motifs, or explicit, as in the case of iconographic sculpture and painting and, in Islamic art and architecture, more often in calligraphy.

The Sufi shrine exemplifies the use and symbolic meaning of ideal forms in architecture. The basic form of a Sufi tomb is a cube chamber topped by a hemispherical dome. The cube symbolizes the earthly, material body, and the dome represents the spiritual, heavenly sphere above. In this metaphor the body of the lover rises upward toward the Beloved, and the Spirit descends halfway to meet it. This meeting of the lover and the Beloved is the *wissal*, the union, the ultimate goal of the Sufi.

The transition from the square to the circle is at once the most challenging and the most intriguing aspect of the tomb's structure and geometry. One method of achieving the transition is to interpose a third element, a zone of transition, between the cube and the sphere. The transition may then be achieved by a series of geometric stages from the square to the octagon to the circle. This third element may appear as a cylindrical neck or drum, or as an octagonal base below the dome. In rare examples, such as the majestic tomb of Shaikh Rukn-i-Alam in Multan, the octagonal form rises directly from the ground, so that on entering the tomb chamber, we are already in the zone of transition. Another device used to make the transition is a series of tiny niches called the *muqarnas*, a marvelous invention that seems to have appeared at about the same time throughout the Islamic world.

From Spain and Morocco to the Middle East, Central Asia, and India, *muqarnases* can be found at the base of domes, in the corners of arched

47

entrances, as cornices and column capitals. The basis is always a complex three-dimensional geometry of half arches and segmented domes forming a honeycomb of niches that corbel one above the other. But each region has its distinct system, and each system allows for an infinite variety of permutations and combinations.

A somewhat related form of articulation is *ghalibkari* or *qalabkari,* a lattice or network of ribs in stucco plaster or brick masonry that is applied to the curved surface of domes and vaults. The typical *ghalibkari* design appears as a starburst. The ribs radiate from the large star at the center, called a *shamsa* or solar motif, often in the form of intersecting helixes that curve down to the base of the dome. At the interstices or nodes are smaller stars, where the ribs now appear as rays emanating from the stars. The whole ensemble makes up a veritable galaxy, spiraling out of an exploding supernova. Once again, the basis of the design is a complex spherical geometry with an infinite variety of applications.

Geometry plays an integral part in the design of Sufi shrines, not only in determining the proportions of the building in plan, section, and elevation, but also in decorative details such as curvilinear arabesques and polygonal *girah* ("knot") patterns. Architecture is thus profoundly connected with the metaphysics of the "sacred" sciences of numbers and geometry.[6] These traditional sciences looked upon phenomena as "effects" whose "cause" was a higher reality, and they enabled man to engage in agriculture, animal husbandry, transportation, and the production of commodities and to establish settled urban communities. In this process of civilization, man saw himself as mediator between "cause" and "effect" and sought to reflect ideal qualities in everything he did and everything he made. Thus, in addition to utility, every object and every act reflected the qualities of beauty. Everything was "art."

The Akhwan al-Safa, the Brotherhood of Purity, was a group of anonymous scholars in the tenth or eleventh century CE (fourth or fifth century AH) who produced a compendium of the arts and sciences in fifty-two epistles that contained a virtual condensation of all knowledge of the time. They placed the science of numbers at the root of all the sciences: "the foundation of wisdom, the source of knowledge and pillar of meaning."[7]

> Know, oh brother … that the study of sensible geometry leads to skill in all the practical arts, while the study of intelligible geometry leads to skill in the intellectual arts because this science is one of the gates through which we move to the knowledge of the essence of the soul, and that is the root of all knowledge …[8]

Thus every form, proportion, and decorative scheme becomes a ground for contemplation of higher realities. Each design is contained by a frame that establishes a finite universe, reflecting a cosmos created in perfect balance and made up of a diversity of elements governed by symmetry and proportion, with a unique center—the origin—to which everything must return. On closer examination, each element turns out to be a microcosmic representation of the larger scheme, with its own frame containing a symmetrical arrangement of elements and a unique center.

The knotted geometric patterns called *girah* are made up of lines woven into nets or webs of constantly changing forms. The spaces between the lines appear now as pattern, now as ground, adding another layer of ambiguity and paradox in the relationship between the apparent (*zahir*) and the hidden (*batin*), between simplicity and complexity. This unveiling or unfolding of the same truth at each level is experienced as one moves toward and through the structures.

In Islamic sacred architecture the center of the wall facing toward Mecca is often provided a prayer niche or *mihrab.* In a mosque the *mihrab* allows the *imam* to stand in front of the congregation without extending the space of the prayer chamber by the width of a whole row, and in a tomb it allows the individual to perform ritual prayer in relative seclusion, undisturbed by the movement of other devotees circulating around the grave of the saint. The *mihrab* is where the Virgin Mary spent her confinement in prayer, and Qur'anic references to the niche make clear its symbolism as the innermost sanctuary, the heart, where one is in the presence of God. In the chapter al Noor (Qur'an 24:35), we read: "Allah is the light of the heavens and the earth. His light is like unto a niche, within it a lamp: the lamp enclosed in glass: the glass as it were a brilliant star, lit from a blessed tree, an olive, neither of the east nor of the west, whose oil is well nigh luminous, though fire touches it not. Light upon light!" Indeed it is here, in this innermost sanctuary, that "the eyes gain sight of the light of God."

Yet another symbol associated with light is the minaret or *minar,* literally a beacon of light that guides the traveler to his goal. In a mosque it provides the elevated platform for the *muezzin* to call the faithful to prayer. In a Sufi tomb a pair of minarets will often flank the entrance, marking the way for the pilgrim; in miniature form, minarets sometimes mark the four corners of the main chamber.

The Sufi shrine is also called a *maqam,* a "station," or a *rawda* or *rauza,* which means a "garden"—and, more specifically, a garden of Paradise. This is to say that the saint, having attained the station of unity with God, is

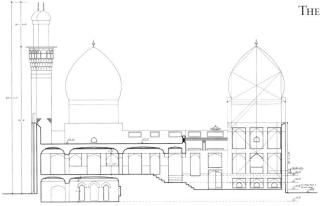

already in Paradise. The Qur'anic word for Paradise is *al-Janna*, which in Arabic means "the garden." The layout, and every detail of the landscape of the classic *chahar bagh* ("four gardens" layout) is based on the Qur'anic description of Paradise as a garden with fountains and canals of flowing water, honey, milk, and wine. The garden itself is a symbol of bliss and delight, while the flowing water, honey, milk, and wine are symbols of four kinds of knowledge: natural, spiritual, intellectual, and sensual. "There will be two gardens … And besides these two there are two other gardens. … In each of them will be two springs pouring forth water in continuous abundance" and "between the two bodies of flowing water is a barrier which they do not transgress" (Qur'an 60:46, 62, 66). Thus we have the four parterres of the *chahar bagh,* with canals and walkways marking the major axes and platforms, fountains, or pavilions at the crossings. In these gardens "will be fruits, and dates and pomegranates" in pairs. The evergreen date palm is a symbol of eternity and the pomegranate of the cycle of life and death, and avenues have alternating pairs of evergreens and blossoming trees. (In different climates the palm is replaced by the cypress and the pomegranate may be substituted by other fruit trees.) Elsewhere the Qur'an tells us that "the people in Paradise will be arranged in ranks": the *mu'mineen* ("those who believe"), the *arifeen* ("those who have knowledge"), and the *muqarribeen* ("those who are the nearest"). The Sufis interpret this to mean first the ranks of ordinary believers, second the Sufis who have attained to the stage of spiritual knowledge, and finally the saints who have attained nearness to God. In the earthly gardens these stages are represented by three ascending terraces, making a rectangle with one long and three shorter axes. The placing of the gates at the head of each axis conforms to the verse that says "the keeper, Ridwan, shall admit them in multitudes through gates, which are eight in number" (Qur'an 15:44).

Placing the tomb inside such a garden is an extravagance usually affordable only under royal patronage. A more common solution is to place the tomb in a "virtual" paradise by decorating its surfaces with floral designs. Indeed, the paradise-garden motif is found throughout the Islamic world, not only in actual gardens but also in carpets, murals, and other visual and plastic arts. Plants, flowers, trees, and fruits are the most obvious allusion to the garden, and each species has its own symbolic meaning. The rose is the epitome of absolute beauty, the sunflower is a solar motif, the grapevine evokes states of ecstasy and intoxication. The cypress, due to its symmetrical form, is a symbol of the perfect man, the *insan e kamil*. With its top bent, however, it becomes a symbol for the submission of the Muslim to God, and with an intertwining vine it represents the lover and the beloved. Two cypresses in a flowerbed symbolize lovers in Paradise. The fruits of Paradise are sometimes shown in a dish, perhaps with a knife cutting into a melon, a reference to the ecstatic effect of the beauty of the prophet Joseph on the ladies of Egypt. The fruit dish is often shown flanked by a pair of wine decanters, a reference to the wine of the purest kind that the inmates of Paradise will be given to drink. As noted above, wine, like water, honey, and milk, is a symbol of knowledge.

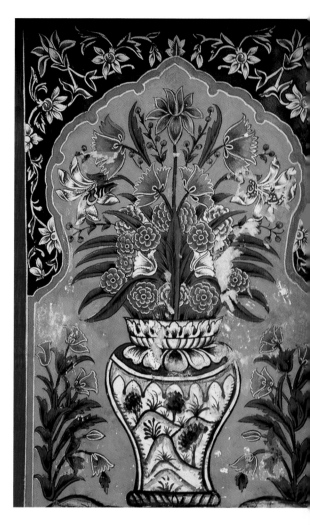

It is not uncommon to find, in the architecture of Sufi shrines, elements borrowed from non-Islamic sources. After all, the basic form of the cube chamber topped by a hemispherical dome is the pre-Islamic *chahar taq* funerary structure found in Sasanian Iran and Balochistan. Here the symbolism of the structure—with its decorations and its high, arched openings oriented toward the four cardinal points or the directions of the four winds—is connected with the four elements of nature: fire, water, air, and earth, which occupy a central place in the Zoroastrian tradition. In South Asia the dome is invariably topped by a *maujbah* and *kalasha,* the inverted lotus and finial of the Hindu *shikhara,* or temple spire. Other such borrowings from Hindu and Buddhist sources include solar symbols such as swastikas and sunflowers, *yantra* geometric patterns, the *padma* lotus symbolizing wisdom and enlightenment, and the trefoil arched niche in which the figure of the deity is replaced by an Arabic inscription, usually the word *Allah.*

These borrowings from local non-Islamic sources, together with adaptations and modifications influenced by climate, materials, and cultural norms, result in the distinctive regional characteristics of Sufi shrines. Yet in all there is a unifying thread, a subtle quality that infuses the diversity of Islamic arts and architectures. Where other traditions may treat the object as allegory or metaphor and "realize" or concretize the metaphysical content in the form of anthropomorphic and naturalistic representations, Islamic art and architecture treat the object as sign or symbol and "idealize" or abstract the floral and other natural forms. Together with proportion, number, and geometry, they thus become the "gates through which we move to the knowledge of the essence of the soul, … the root of all knowledge."[9] But the most efficient vehicle for the communication of this knowledge

is the word—spoken, as in the recitation of the Qur'an, or written, as in calligraphy.

Abul Fazal, the court historian of Akbar the Great, discusses in some detail the superiority of calligraphy over representational art in a section on the painting studios in the *A'een e Akbari*.[10]

… the likeness of the body is drawn in the picture, which is well known, and the European artists enable the spectators to roam the cloisters of reality, by bringing forth strange and wondrous forms in innumerable creative manners and styles, so that the eye is deceived into taking the likeness for the real. But writing has a far loftier and superior status because it informs us of the experiences of ancient masters, and the intellect and understanding is developed by this intimacy …

The best form of illustration is calligraphy. …Those who are attracted by outer appearances only regard the written word as a black form, but those who can discern the truth understand it as a lamp of discernment. …

It is an imprint of the Divine handiwork, a product from the domain of truth and spirituality. It is a night in which the sun is radiant and manifest. It is a dark cloud from which are raining radiant and brilliant pearls. It is the treasure of sight and the secret chamber of reality. It is a strange and wonderful talisman that speaks in a world of silence …

Its reality is that of a beam from the divine torch of knowledge that falls on the articulate soul. The heart conveys this beam to the imaginal world, which is intermediate between the abstract and the material worlds, so that the abstract may establish a relationship with the material, and an absolute entity may become accustomed to the bonds of confinement.

After this stage the beam descends from the celestial imaginal world to the heart, and comes from the heart to the tongue, and from the tongue enters the ear through the air, and after this, freeing itself from material ties one after the other, returns to its real center.

Sometimes it so happens that this celestial traveler is aided by the fingertips to tour the land and sea of pen and ink, and having completed its excursion, is brought down to the parlor of the page of white paper.

This celestial guest flies off to the higher world by way of the eyes, leaving its footprint on the sheets of paper.

Inscriptions on the tombs may include Qur'anic texts, *hadith* sayings of the Prophet, verses from the buried saint or by other Sufi poets. These texts are carefully selected to convey particular meanings relevant to the saint in question, his character, spiritual station, and teachings. A typical example is the Persian inscription over the entrance of the tomb of Hadrat Ali Hujwiri in Lahore, which may be translated as "Bestower of treasures, of grace and munificence to the world, the manifestation of the Light of God. The perfect mentor to the less-than-perfect, a guide for the perfected ones."

Over the last twenty years or so my colleagues and I have been endeavoring to understand the building practices and design theories that have formed the basis of traditional architecture in Pakistan. One thing that has become clear to us in this process is the profound connection between traditional arts and crafts and the metaphysical and idealist worldview of traditional societies. But understanding the intellectual content and theoretical basis is one thing; putting it into practice is quite another.[11]

Two essential components of the traditional design method in Islam are proportioning and the use of "ideal forms." The system of proportional subdivision, as a method of design, had intrigued me for a long time. But such mundane obstacles as building regulations had proved, in practice, to be insurmountable. Equally, although our clients have generally been very supportive of our ideas, we had not found anyone willing to realize them fully in terms of design principles, building materials, and construction techniques. But in fact the greatest barrier had been my own education and training as an architect. The compulsion to be innovative, to be creative, to be original, the imperative to be "expressive of our time," had always stopped me short of what could be seen as imitation and copying. In the final analysis, my ego simply refused to let go, to surrender. Only recently have I been able to cross this barrier under the guidance of a spiritual master—Shaikh Abu Bakr Siraj-ed-Din. In the two current projects discussed here I have been able to apply the traditional design method for the first time in my own work.

The projects are a mosque and a tomb. The mosque is located outside a small Pakistani town in the district of Mandi Bahauddin, about 150 kilometers west of Lahore. The tomb is actually two tombs for a "hidden" Sufi and his master. They are located near the Shalimar Gardens in Lahore.

The site of the mosque is known locally as Pak Wigah, or "sacred field." The land records mark it as a pilgrimage site, and it is mentioned in several histories and private documents as the spot where a waking vision of the Prophet was witnessed by a gathering of hundreds of Sufis, including some of the most distinguished sages of the time, in 1739. The client for this

mosque is Dr. Sahibzada Mohammed Farakh Hafeez, an eye surgeon who is also a shaikh of a Sufi order (*tariqa*) known as the Naushahi and who has a devoted following in his area. He traces his spiritual and family ancestry back to the saint who presided over the gathering of Sufis in 1739.

The clients for the tombs are two young engineers who run a construction firm in Lahore. They belong to the inner circle of friends and admirers of a remarkable saintly person, Hafiz Mohammad Iqbal, who died on 20 November 2001 and was buried in the same compound as his equally remarkable master, Baba Hasan Din, who died in 1968 at the age of a hundred and six. Hafiz Iqbal left a promising academic career—he had three M.A. degrees and a teaching position at the Government College in Lahore—to spend his life in relative seclusion. British-born Hasan Din was named Alfred Victor by his British father and French mother. A Sufi of the Awwal Qadir order, he was employed as a mechanical engineer for British Railways before leaving England under the spiritual guidance of the eleventh-century saint Ali Hujwiri. Hasan Din spent forty years in the forests of Kenya before he settled in Lahore.

These clients came to my architectural firm because they wanted strictly traditional buildings using traditional materials and structural systems. In each case there was also a clearly stated desire that the designs be based on specific historic structures: the Moti Masjid in the Delhi fort, in the case of the mosque, and the shrine of Imam Ali, the cousin and son-in-law of the Prophet, at Najaf in Iraq, in the case of the tombs.

Had these gentlemen come to me a few months earlier I would have shown them the door. I would have felt insulted at being asked to copy or even borrow from an existing building. "Was I not capable," I would have thought, "of creating and evolving out of the logic of the site and functional requirements, the most appropriate forms?" But I had reached a point in my own understanding of traditional design theory where I could accept these requests as perfectly normal, indeed necessary to the design process. We were able to find some published drawings and photographs of the two monuments, our clients downloaded other images from the Internet, and we then proceeded to analyze this material—photographs, plans, elevations, and sections—to decode the underlying proportioning systems and geometries. These we applied to the particular sites and adjusted to the functional requirements of the clients. Following the traditional design method, we proceeded by proportionate subdivisions—of the whole site in the case of the tombs and of the designated area for the mosque—to establish the basic structural and planning grids. The same procedure was used to arrive at the basic features of the elevations and sections.

The designs thus prepared were "approved" by a curious process in each case. The eye surgeon had often said that *he* was not making the project, that it was making itself—implying that a higher force was guiding the project at each stage. Thus, he said he was both led to the architect and shown the prototype. At critical stages he would take our designs and return a few days later to inform us that they had either been "approved" or not. At one stage, for instance, we told him that the proportions of the Delhi mosque appeared more suited for a royal chapel but seemed too tall and imposing for our humbler rural context. He said he had been wanting to tell us the same thing. So we tried out several shorter versions. None of these were "approved," however, and we had to revert to the original proportions. For the courtyard of the mosque, we were asked to modify the original scheme by eliminating the ablution tank and by increasing the length, to conform to the mysteriously "approved" design.

In the case of the tombs, our design had been immediately accepted by the circle of friends of Hafiz Iqbal, but the old caretaker and devotee of Baba Hasan Din had maintained an ominous silence. We had no inkling of what this meant until the day our clients, the two engineers, came into the office radiant with joy and gave us the "good news" that the design had been "approved" by the higher authority. "Go ahead," Baba Hasan Din's caretaker had told them. "You have been permitted. You may build a temple, a church, or a mosque. I am not to stand in your way."

In both cases we were led to correct fundamental mistakes in the design by strange coincidences. The doctor had already decided on the size of the prayer chamber for the mosque before he came to us. In fact, he had even started excavations for the foundation. So it came as a bit of a surprise when we found that the outline of his plan matched exactly the basic rectangle of the Delhi prototype. But when the site engineer started laying out our plan on the ground, he found that it did not fit the foundation prepared by Dr. Hafeez. We checked the measurements on site, and rechecked our plans. That was when we realized we had gone horribly astray! Somewhere, while playing around with different proportions, we had locked onto the wrong proportioning system, based on the square root of two, instead of the square root of three. In fact, we thought we had discovered the underlying design principle and could now freely improvise. Fortunately, we were stopped in the nick of time from producing a grotesque parody of the original. Suitably humbled, we gave up further attempts at willful invention and returned to faithful copying. I had learned a valuable lesson in keeping the ego in check. The project was indeed designing itself.

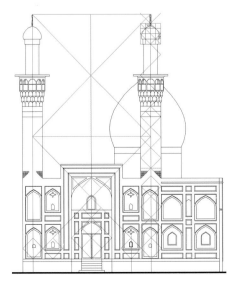

In the case of the tombs, the site had been measured by the engineers, then checked and double-checked at our insistence. But when we set out our plan on the site, we discovered a huge discrepancy between the size of the plot on the ground and the measurements originally provided us. We went back to the drawing board. Once again, we realized that we had been using the wrong proportioning system that would have resulted in a badly stunted version of the prototype.

This sort of "copying" and working from prescribed models is never, in practice, simply a mechanical process of reproduction. It involves intelligent interpretation, adaptation, and application of critical judgment and discernment at every step of the way. As Pakistani master mason Ustad Haji Abdul Aziz would put it, "I can give you all the formulas, the ratios, and proportions for every element, but there always comes a point when the craftsman has to exercise his imagination. It is a question of *hawa* [lit. "air"; in design the term refers to the subtleties of form]. This is a subtle quality. It cannot be defined. You have to let your eye and your heart guide you."

Location, the size and shape of the site, adjoining properties, public road access, user profiles, available materials, local climate, and so on, are just some of the factors that called for modifications, adaptations, and design decisions in both of these projects. Unlike the royal chapel blocked in between the other structures in the Delhi fort complex, our mosque, located in the open fields, had to be raised on a very high plinth. Instead of a small private entrance for the king, we needed a prominent grand entrance for the public. The somber solidity of the outer wall had to be made more permeable to light and ventilation, and the Delhi sandstone had to be replaced by a lighter colored marble.

Similarly, our site in a modest urban neighborhood of Lahore, and the simple functional requirements for the twin tombs, bore no resemblance to the monumental tomb in the middle of a sprawling complex in Iraq. So, while we were able to borrow the basic forms and proportions of the central dome, the two principle entrances, and the minarets, the sizes had to be reduced to the scale of our project. Moreover, the plan had to be entirely reconceived around the locations of the existing graves and a small row of trees planted by Hafiz Iqbal himself. Another factor was the location of the site in the old flood plain of the Ravi River, which had been cut off from the present riverbed by a protection embankment, later turned into a landfill site for the city, and finally developed as a residential area in recent times.

Both of these projects are now well underway. We are using the age-old materials of bricks and lime mortar and have revived the traditional

formula using *kankar* or *kasuri chuna*—a naturally occurring hydraulic lime found in the shape of spongelike nodules all over the Punjab plains. The mosque project is of particular interest because lime kilns, a grinding mill, and a stone-cutting facility have all been built on-site and the building will be clad, both internally and externally, in elaborately carved marble. The exterior of the tomb complex will include *kashikari*—reviving the unique Lahori art of glazed tile mosaics, whose last recognized master died some fifty years ago—and *tazakari,* or imitation brick. On the interior the *kankar* lime plaster will be finished with fine lime *pukka kali.* The decorative schemes include stone carving, stone inlay, plaster relief (*thoba* and *ghalibkari*), fresco (*naqqashi*), and wood carving using geometric and floral forms and, of course, calligraphy. Our clients play the major role in selecting the texts and their locations, but the whole design process is a close collaboration between architects, clients, and craftsmen. Ustad Khursheed Alam Gauhar Qalam and Ahmad Ali Bhutta are the calligraphers on the projects.

Something quite extraordinary has happened at the mosque in the last two years. The designs call for quite a lot of marble carving, and the client had gone to great effort to locate a group of skilled masons and set up their workshop on the site. Their output was very slow, so he got a second team and built another workshop for them. However, the combined output of the two teams was still too slow, so finally both were sent packing. And then, a miracle happened. One hundred stonecarvers materialized out of nowhere to take up the work. Twice a week, they appear after dark and work through the night. The site is ablaze with powerful lights. The music of hymns and chants playing over the loudspeakers all but drowns the din of more than forty power tools. The air is filled with marble dust that turns everything chalky white—white hair, white faces with cut-out liquid eyes and tracks of joyful tears running down the cheeks. At the break of dawn, the work stops, the carvers say their morning prayers in congregation, and then disperse. Washed and changed, they step into the day as ordinary teachers, lawyers, paramedics, and shopkeepers and go about their daily routines.

Not one of these men had held a mason's tool in his hands before. The venerable surgeon himself has become not only an accomplished draftsman but a remarkable calligrapher as well. With no previous training in the art, he began one day to compose the required texts in an entirely new script, perfectly balanced and proportionate, clearly the result of pure inspiration. He draws directly on the stone. One team cuts out the stencils, a second team does the rough shaping, a third the fine chiseling, a fourth the

polishing and finishing. Each section is assembled dry and checked before being placed on site by a professional mason. Among this new workforce are several teenagers who were sent to work on the project by their parents to keep them out of trouble. These formerly wayward youths have blossomed into fine and utterly devoted craftsmen.

The transformative nature of these projects is something we have experienced not only in our own work as designers, but equally in the lives and attitudes of clients, builders, craftsmen, and ordinary visitors. Whether this is due to the quality of the architecture or the association of these places with holy relics, pious persons, or the performance of religious rites, there is no doubt that these spaces make us intensely aware of the presence of the Divine.

Notes

1. From an extract from "Muqamaat I Dawoodi" by Abdul Baqi, included in appendix 2 of the monograph "Ahwal al Sheikh Dawood Jhunniwal," an Urdu translation of a thesis by Mohammad Haidar, written in March 1931 and privately published by Sayyid Mohammed Mohsin in Lahore (n.d.). English translation by the author, previously published in his book *Modernity and Tradition*.
2. The *mandala* and *yantra* are cosmic diagrams in the Buddhist and Hindu traditions, used in ritual and sacred art and architecture. The *hasht bihisht* is a three-by-three "magic square" with eight squares around the central one. Literally, it means "eight paradises," and it forms the basis of the plans for many Islamic buildings, including tombs.
3. For a detailed description of this term, see Chittick, *Imaginal Worlds,* 25, 52–54, 99.
4. See the Introduction to Martin Lings, *Sufi Poems,* where he maintains that true artistic creativity requires an action of the Spirit.
5. See Martin Lings, "The Seven Deadly Sins in the Light of the Symbolism of Number."
6. See Critchlow, *Islamic Patterns.*
7. Ibid., 42.
8. Ibid., 7.
9. Ibid., 5.
10. Fazal, *A'een e Akbari.* Some of this section of text is adapted from a seminar on "Culture and Calligraphy" given by the author on 20 November 2007.
11. The following section is adapted from a paper presented at a Prasada conference in 2002 at De Montfort University, UK.

I was a Hidden Treasure,
so I loved to be known.
Hence I created
the Creation that
I might be known.

Hadith Qudsi

كُنْتُ كَنْزاً مَخْفِيّاً فَأَحْبَبْتُ أَنْ
أُعْرَفَ فَخَلَقْتُ الخَلْقَ لِأُعْرَفَ

STORYTELLING AS IMAGINATIVE HISTORY

SAMINA QURAESHI

In each part of the world where Islam has spread and taken root, the religion has adapted to its context in geographic, cultural, and theological terms. Sufism, the mystical dimension of Islam, runs through South Asia as a deep spiritual vein inflected with philosophies and traditions from other Muslim lands and cultures and with pre-Islamic rites and practices. Sufi mysticism is one of many nuances that complicate the all-too-common view that Islam is monolithic—unable or unwilling to recognize the internal plurality of devotion and interpretation among its faithful. This book is a personal and artistic act of resistance against those forces—both within Islam and outside of it—that seek to deny such nuances, to silence the voices of mystics, and to distill the diversity of Islamic piety into something essential, unitary, and uniform. I rely on memory, storytelling, and image making to distill an understanding from the many facets of Islam's mystical dimensions.

Political commentators too often categorize diverse conflicts erupting across our world today—a cacophony of violence that includes such diverse actors as national and local governments, global corporations, radical fanatics, guerilla insurgents, nationalist paramilitaries, venal criminals, and countless innocent civilians—as evidence of what Samuel Huntington has called a clash of civilizations. In this view, the voice of fundamentalist Islam eclipses all others within Muslim communities, collapsing diverse ethnic identities from Malay to Moroccan into the image of a jihadist. In fact, there is no singular or cohesive "Muslim world," but rather a vast network of communities that stretches from China and Indonesia to Nigeria and from Bradford, England, and Kreuzberg, Germany, to Dearborn, Michigan. It is made up of many ethnicities, languages, and nationalities, and many different interpretations of the Holy Qur'an.

Bird's-eye view of the Old City, Lahore.
Unknown artist and date.

69

My home country of Pakistan is a significant pressure point in the political and religious turmoil that envelops contemporary Islam. Yet when I look back at the Pakistan I knew growing up, I see a region energized by independent-minded people—a place filled with anomalies and contradictions, but also infused with ancient traditions, codes of honor, and deep beliefs that were allowed to coexist in the natural order of things. I recall a time when the people of the Indus Valley were proud of their continuous history of fifty-five centuries of civilization and the different spiritual traditions manifested in our devotional practices. The Indus Valley is a palimpsest of history, culture, and geography, as well as a crossroads of explorations, civilizations, and religions. And so this region, where Islam overlaps Hinduism, Sikhism, Jainism, Christianity, and Buddhism, is rife with stories of miracles and allegiances to *shaikh*s, *pir*s, *faqir*s, and dervishes dedicated to seeking unity with the Divine and serving mankind.

It is sometimes forgotten that Sufism was spread in South Asia from the ninth century onward by Sufi teachers, known as *shaikh*s, who originated in Iraq, Iran, and Central Asia. Many of these religious teachers migrated to Sindh, Punjab, Rajasthan, Delhi, Bihar, Bengal, and the Deccan, where, in the twelfth and thirteenth centuries of the Christian era (CE), they established Sufi fraternities such as the Chishti, Suhrawardi, Qadiri, Firdausi, Qubrawi, Shattari, and the Naqshbandi.

These *silsila*s, or schools (literally, "chains"), of religious interpretation and their devotional practices are alive and well in South Asia today, with estimates of up to two-thirds of the total populations of India and Pakistan claiming allegiance to one *dargah* (shrine) or another. Exploring contemporary engagement with the sacred spaces of Sufi practices in South Asia is not intended to present a soft and sentimental foil to the reductive

image of Islamic fundamentalism. On the contrary, the mystical dimension is immanent within and intrinsic to Islamic faith.

Yet when I return to Pakistan now, I see a conscious diminishing of these practices, a willing erasure of South Asian rites in favor of new interpretations of piety prescribed by the more conservative elements of Islam. The spiritual avenues are blocked, and I wonder why. I see relatives embarrassed by the Hindu inflections of our weddings and dismissing the mystical dimension inherent in pilgrimages as mere superstition. I remember celebrating the uniqueness of Islam in South Asia while enjoying the opportunity to explore the different experience of Muslim life in Turkey or Egypt or Malaysia. But now I am forced to ask myself, Why aren't the teachings of the Sufi sages I had been brought up with continuing to inspire a renewed sense of our common obligation to one another, to our communities, to our world? Have their inspired teachings been deliberately suppressed in the striving for a "pure" Islam? And what of the mystical music and poetry that were so much a part of our cultural understanding? Why are the spiritual aspects of the Sufi tradition not helping people to achieve a sense of spiritual peace and well being? Or providing the faithful an alternative to fanaticism? Or guiding them toward personal connections to the Divine?

I believe that exposure to the historical context of Islamic cultural development is the best means to counter the violent ways in which Islam is being redefined by fundamentalists to mean something it was never meant to mean. When I encounter extremists, I have to examine what makes them so radical and so alien to me, a Muslim woman. The currents of history and the deeper ones of religion are so deeply intertwined that to discover what they mean required that I embark on a personal quest that would begin with revisiting the faith-based nature of these ritual practices.

Sensing that the rules and laws and politicization of Islam have allowed the mystical dimensions to be ignored, I wanted to find the custodians of the wisdom of the Sufi mystics whose teachings compel me to rethink issues that affect us all, from the mundane to the sublime.

Spirituality resists easy definitions. I was taught that understanding the correct outer expression would help achieve the desired inner reality, and this remains a challenge given myriad practices, disciplines, and cultural differences. The guiding lights of Islam—the Holy Qur'an, the eternal book of Allah, the teachings of the Prophet Muhammad, and the religious law that is *sharia*—have to be studied with religious specialists in order to understand the diversity of resources and worldviews. What is the common Islamic experience?

Experiencing the living tradition embodied by the expressions and enactments of the shaikhs' teachings at some of the Sufi sanctuaries of the Indus region would inform my own understanding and shed light on the complex relationship between place, symbol, idea, and oral tradition in Islamic mysticism. Mosques, *madrasah*s, and hospices are often associated with the shrine complexes of the more renowned Sufis, where the most celebrated ritual, the annual *urs* festival, marks the death anniversary of the shaikh. The *urs* celebrates the shaikh's departing soul uniting with the Divine, a symbolic sacred wedding. It is at these festivals that pilgrims, especially women, come pouring in from all over the country and abroad. Voluntary donations from the pilgrims feed all those who gather here: acts of patronage that are said to benefit the giver with the *baraka*, the spiritual grace of the shaikh. The devotional practices of the mystics and their followers were the power behind this outpouring of dedication and charity in the lives of the faithful. I wanted to be a part of the *urs*, to experience the recitations of mystic poetry and the ecstatic *qawwali*s, to abandon myself to the entranced state that the chanting inspires, and to participate in acts of devotion to the saints.

The most important element that binds the Indus Valley Sufi traditions together and that provides the tradition with its life blood is participation in age-old rituals. All the great saints of the Indus Valley, such as Shah Abdul Latif, Data Ganj Bakhsh, Rukn-i-Alam, Bulleh Shah, Mian Mir, and Madho Lal Husain, have left behind a spiritual legacy. Pilgrims still believe that the spirits of these shaikhs live on, guiding people through the ritual performances and attuning them to the spiritual principles that each shaikh practiced. Whether it is recitations from the Qur'an, remembrances of the Prophet Muhammad, recitation of the names of Allah through the *zikr*, the distribution of food outside Bulleh Shah's shrine in Lahore, fasting for many days, commemoration of Shah Abdul Latif's birthday, or visitation by pilgrims to Data Sahib's shrine, all these acts of piety articulate the commitment of Sufi wayfarers to the spiritual and mystical authority and legacy of their heroic masters, their shaikhs.

Each founder of a Sufi lineage epitomized in his life the teachings and practices named after him. The practice of obedience to the master was understood as a renouncing of the ego by the disciple, who accepted and respected the master's will. The master was known as the elder shaikh or *pir* or *khwaja*—all terms meaning lord, leader, or master. The memory and imagined spiritual grace of the original masters and of each successive master serves as the fountainhead for the lay Sufi practitioner's religious inspiration. In this sense, embedded in Sufi practice is a historical memory available to those who link themselves to the original Sufi masters through their *malfuzat*, or teachings, their *khanqahs*, or seminaries, and the discipline of submitting one's will to God. Parables, allegories, and anecdotes are essential ingredients of the teachings, and the most evocative aspect of Sufism's living tradition can be found enacted at the shrines and mausoleums of Sufi shaikhs. The music and dance performed by devotees is an integral ritual at the *dargahs* and is considered to be an act of surrender to God. Pilgrims believe that *sama* (an assembly where *qawwali* or dance is performed) heightens the spiritual sensibilities.

Each shaikh is a spiritual master who has walked on the *tariqa*, the Sufi Way, and evolved his own path to spiritual self-knowledge. He is a guide who can lead pilgrims to the divine reality of God. The *silsilas* represent the many paths that lead to this goal. A teaching these shaikhs share is the emphasis on the love of all humanity regardless of caste, creed, age, sex, color, or religion. That is common to all. Another hallmark of the Sufi tradition is its strong emphasis on the importance of master–disciple relationships that helped cultivate Sufism as a set of social institutions. Indeed, Sufism can be thought of as the intergenerational transmission of

values, norms, and beliefs by charismatic authorities. Sufis follow the

A prince with his tutor. Mughal, c. eighteenth century CE.

guidance provided by God in the Qur'an, but most people in this region also have allegiance to a particular shaikh and to the shrine associated with him.

Sufism is today a vast network that spans the globe, punctuated by sanctuaries saturated with the spiritual power that their pilgrims seek. I thought my own visits to the shrines might tell me whether this tradition is as important now as it has been since the first shaikhs began to share their vision of a more charitable world some 1,200 years ago. How does this practice play out in unique ways in specific social contexts where an individual religious interpretation has intersected with the infinite layers of a particular local culture? How does the unity derived from a universal love for God translate in the contemporary spiritual and physical geography of the region today?

In looking to my upbringing, I am reminded that the living traditions of pilgrimage, homage, love, longing, and spiritual quest expressed in Sufi poems and songs informed my life. Having guides to life's journey was enriched by both depth of historical continuity and the continuous evolutionary changes to ritual and interpretation. At this troubled time, looking back through a lens of personal memory rather than canonical history is a vital step toward countering more narrow-minded modes of historicism. The first step involves reclaiming storytelling as a viable model of imaginative history. Some of the stories I tell here have sources in the literature on Sufism. Others have their source in the ever-changing oral traditions of the people of South Asia, the family and friends and spiritual teachers of my homeland.

The ecstasy of the heart is deeper than the
seas and the oceans
As the ships house the sea, so does the
entirety of creation live inside the human
heart
But only that human heart that is besieged
by divine love
Only he who knows the secret of the heart
can comprehend the divine truth
    Sultan Bahu

ھُو

دل دریا سمندروں ڈوگھے کون دلاں دیاں جانے ھُو

وچے بیڑے وچے جھیڑے وچے وَنجھ مُہانے ھُو

چودھاں طبق دلے دے اندر جتھے عشق تمبو دی وچ تانے ھُو

جو دل دا محرم ہووے باھُو سوئی رب پچھانے ھُو

سُلطان باھُو

In the chaotic joint family of my upbringing, stories were a matter of survival. My father, Abdus Sattar Quraeshi, had three wives and ten children: eight boys, and two girls. I was one of the middle children. We lived with our father's mother, an aunt and her son, and various other relatives who came for extended visits. In India, my father's three households had been separate nuclear families who lived in different states. But the violent shock of Partition in 1947 threw us together into a loving mélange of mothers, aunts, and grandmothers, each unfamiliar with the strange land of Pakistan and unsure of her role in the new household.

My own historical imagination was awakened in the context of the home; my spiritual journey began in that most domestic of realms. Servants structured my family's daily routine—a cook, a bearer, an *ayah* or nanny: Everyone was a refugee from a different part of India and all were Muslim, having left their homes for a new beginning in Pakistan. Each had command of one of the day's episodes, and our life was inextricably tied to their activities. Our servants ordinarily performed their tasks silently, but when their adult employers were elsewhere they stopped to talk to the children and each other. I loved their stories, tales about their villages and the people they had left behind. The tales conjured up these lost memories.

In the servants' quarters I was treated as an honored guest. Seated cross-legged on a *charpoy* or string-cot, I savored their hot milky tea, a much more pungent brew than the one my mother served, and devoured their stories. My questions were generally answered through parables. In this way, I was introduced to the oral tradition—the life-blood of our culture. Though poor, many of these men and women had crossed oceans and seen worlds far beyond my own. Majid, the "majordomo" of our household, came to India as an indentured servant to the *nawab* (ruler) of the princely state of Junagadh and found his way to our family through an elaborate network of servants. His stories were my favorites, for he was able to imbue them with a sense of wonder, of a world with no limits or boundaries. He would modulate his voice to conjure up evil djinns, beautiful princesses, and singing angels in our living room. He believed that countries were artificial constructs and that true pilgrims wandered the world at will. His people, he told us, were highly regarded by the ruling families, including the Mughals and the Marathas, and had served in roles ranging from military generals to close confidants. We regarded Majid as a member of our extended family, and we children were asked by the adults to treat him with the respect that his responsibilities in our household commanded.

When we asked Majid how he could conjure up visions through his voice and transport us into distant realms, he told us that at the time of the Prophet Muhammad there was a slave from Africa who was called Bilal. While at work near Medina, he heard the Prophet speak and was so moved

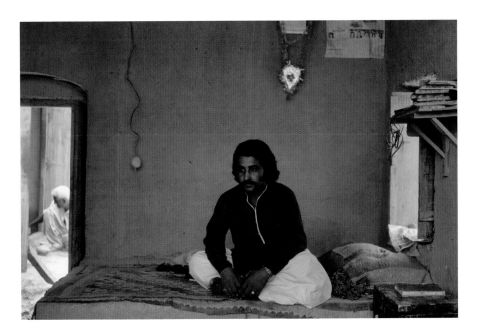

that he was among the first to accept Islam. Bilal had a strong faith in Allah and a great love for the Prophet, which he expressed by reciting the Qur'an in his melodious voice. He became a close companion of Muhammad, earning his respect and also that of the other great Muslims of the time. The Prophet appreciated Bilal's powerful sweet voice and made him the first *muezzin*—The Caller to the Prayers.

"Are you related to Bilal, Majid?" we asked.

He answered, "Perhaps. True relationships come from the love of other human beings. You are my family because you love me and respect me, and we are all beloved by God."

We realized he was telling us this story to illustrate that talents and abilities, combined with imagination, could allow a slave to become a worthy companion of the Holy Prophet, just as Majid had become a respected member of our family even though he was a servant.

He continued, "To see through this world, we have been given our imaginations, and you must look beyond symbols and signs. Close your eyes and see with your heart." This was the first inkling I had that true power comes from the ability to transform a mundane reality into worlds beyond horizons.

In the 1960s, Karachi was a vibrant city full of optimism. The majority population was Sunni Muslim, but people from several different ethnic and religious communities lived around us. Our Zoroastrian (Parsi) neighbors invited us to join them each year for Nauroze, their celebration of the New

81

Year. Our Christian friends opened their homes to us for lively parties at Christmas and Easter. We had close relationships with some of the Jewish families who still lived in Karachi. Many were related to my mother's family in India, and they invited us to join in on the Jewish holidays, their weddings and bar mitzvahs, and other celebrations. Nearby lived a Hindu family who had chosen to remain in Pakistan instead of moving to the newly independent India. Despite the tension between Hindus and Muslims in the region, these friends were always willing to answer my many childish questions about their pantheon of gods.

My father sent all of his children to schools run by Catholic missionaries, never worrying that the religious education his children received at home would be threatened by this exposure to non-Muslim teachings. He told us that the Jews and Christians were *Ahl al-Kitab*, or "People of the Book," who received scriptures prior to Muhammad. The Talmud of the Jews and the Bible of the Christians are the central religious texts of these religions, and the Qur'an is taken to represent the completion of these scriptures. We would benefit by studying all three.

My school, St. Joseph's Convent, was established by a Catholic order in 1862 and was run by nuns who taught us all the required subjects. All the boys went to St. Patrick's School, where they were taught by Catholic priests. Every weekday, our driver would pull the family car around Q House, our family home, to take my older sister, Sajida, and me to school, dressed in our starched uniforms. We wore pleated frocks with sky-blue collars and cuffs and a patch pocket embroidered with "SJC." Conceived by the nuns to replicate what they remembered from their childhoods in far-off Britain, the uniforms were ill suited to life in Karachi. Conscientious Muslim and Hindu parents, squeamish about standards of modesty, insisted that their daughters wear white *shalwars*, or pantaloons, beneath the required pleated skirt. The resulting ensemble was odd, bulky, and unable to withstand the blazing heat, which would reduce our jumpers to limp, wrinkled sacks by mid-morning. But Sister Dolores Ann ignored our disheveled look as she briskly led the music hour every morning and taught us to sing hymns and chant "Hail Mary, full of grace …"

At home we observed the Muslim way of life, practicing the prescribed rituals of faith and charity and learning from our holy book, the Qur'an, so that we would be guided by its principles. Friday prayers were an important part of our week. The women of the family spread white sheets over the carpets on the front verandah, and when we heard the *azan*, or call to prayer, we all gathered together to face Mecca and offer our prayers. Praying together created a bond between us. Lined up on the carpet, facing Mecca, we felt one before God and part of the *ummah*, the larger Muslim worldwide community, which was united by this symbolic act. For a time, all arguments and differences were forgotten.

After the call to prayers, the men of the family went to the neighborhood mosque and listened to the *maulvi*, the religious scholar who leads the congregation in prayer. Once they returned, we ate together. A portion of our meal was always sent to the mosque to feed the poor; my father was determined to continue the tradition his family had followed in their ancestral home of Ajmer. For my father, the interplay between national pride in Pakistan, his adopted and newly created country, and homesickness for the place of his birth in Ajmer was complex. And it served to create another powerful influence in our multivalent identities.

My family had come to Karachi from Ajmer, in Rajasthan, in 1947, amid the widespread chaos and bloodshed wrought by the demise of the British Empire in India and the Partition that created Independent India and Pakistan. Once a sleepy seaside village, Karachi grew overnight into a sprawling city, its population swelled by *muhajirs*, or migrants, from India. My father's family had lived in India for generations. They were based in Rajasthan and Bombay, enjoying successful business and social relationships with people of various religious groups. But in the tense days leading up to the Partition of India, some of those relationships turned sour. Everyday exchanges between friends of different ethnic and religious backgrounds were replaced by bickering and harsh remarks over religion and family bloodlines. Then the riots began.

My father witnessed Sikhs slaughtering Muslims, Hindus butchering Muslims, and Muslims burning Hindus alive. He saw men betraying one another across all religious lines. Rising tensions were inflamed with reports of murder, rape, and rioting mobs wrecking homes, shops, temples, and mosques. Heartbroken at the impasse between the political parties and out of fear for his family's safety, my father reluctantly decided to leave for Pakistan. He decided that we would settle in Karachi—his sisters were married into local families in Sindh, and therefore we could escape the hastily assembled refugee camps that were set up to accommodate lost travelers and the hundreds of thousands that fled the familiar for an unknown land. The family was gathered together from the different estates and boarded a steamship from Bombay to Karachi. So began the attempt to carve out a life in the new country. Karachi's streets became crowded as new areas around it were developed. New and old confronted each other, ethnicities, cultures, and languages made a wild cacophony, and the transformation of what had been a small fishing village by the sea was irrevocable.

One day, shortly after we had arrived, a woman I came to know as Ustaniji ("teacher") appeared at our doorstep without warning, direct from one of the refugee camps. She had heard that my father and she were both exiled from Ajmer. Ustaniji came from a family of Sufis and was learned in Persian and Arabic. I remember her so vividly. She was attractive, with delicate features. Her black hair was pulled severely into a plait that was covered by the *dupatta*, a scarf she wore over her shoulders and head. She had a small diamond in her nose that sparkled as she moved her head while talking. She always wore cotton *tang* pajamas under her long *kameez*, a narrow white dress. Clean and compact, she exuded an air of serenity despite her straightened economic circumstances and her grief at being alone. Ustaniji told my father that she was related to the *khadim*s, a family of caretakers who are custodians and spiritual guides at the shrine of Shaikh Muinuddin Chishti. During the Partition, she had become separated from her family. The chaos was overwhelming, she could not remember which *qafila*, or caravan, they were in, and she was carried forward by a tide of refugees. Now she was trying to contact relatives who might have reached Karachi. Having been raised in the complex that surrounds the shrine, Ustaniji was well versed in the history of this great Sufi teacher and his legacy. Impressed by her knowledge and ability to communicate, Father hired her to be his children's religious instructor.

As a young girl, I was always hungry for ways to escape. I found my refuge in the servants' quarters and in long conversations with Ustaniji,

my religious tutor. The stories she told me of miracles that Sufis performed and folk tales that were parables for the Sufi Way provided me a historical and theological framework: the layering of individual life narratives and devotional practices gave rise to my personal relationship with Islam and my personal journey as a Muslim.

Ustaniji arrived every afternoon to teach us how to read the Qur'an and perform our daily prayers. *Bismillah ur-rahman ur-rahim* ("In the name of Allah the beneficent and merciful"), she would begin, before imploring me to "Read, my child, read! There are thirty parts and we must get started."

Sometimes Ustaniji would allow us to take a break from reading the Qur'an and tell us a folktale. She loved singing pieces of the verses of mystical poems that were the basis of the story. She sang of Heer, the peerless beauty from the Punjab who loved Ranjha. "Heer represents the soul," she told us, "and Ranjha the Divine Beloved." She taught us that stories are parables and that there are mysteries wrapped in the words that we could imagine and unravel ourselves. To be sure, her teachings were rooted in the holiest text of Islam, but her lessons extended to the interpretations of the stories of great Sufi sages and their ballads.

My exposure in school to Christian thinking was at times difficult to reconcile with Ustaniji's lessons. Shortly after she began tutoring us, I went to my father to ask whether I would go to hell if I prayed to Allah, whom I learned about at home, instead of to God, whom I learned about in school. Allah, my father explained, was the same as God. He reminded me that the People of the Book could even marry without conversion because there was no compulsion to convert within Islam. "Let there be no compulsion in religion," it says in the Qur'an (2:256). "Truth stands out clear from error; whoever rejects evil and believes in Allah hath grasped the most trustworthy hand-hold that never breaks. And Allah heareth and knoweth all things." I was relieved. From that point on, I would come home after participating enthusiastically in the nuns' rituals and feel grateful that my father had taught us to believe that all paths lead to God.

I soon learned that the significance of Ajmer did not rest exclusively in the fact that it was the ancestral home to both my father's and Ustaniji's families. There was something special about this faraway place in India to which we, as Pakistanis, now had limited access. For my father and for Ustaniji, Ajmer held a special power. Of course, all of us faced in the opposite direction when we prayed: we turned west toward faraway Mecca, not east to India. Even Bethlehem, Jerusalem, and Rome, the sacred cities I learned about at school, were distant sites that hosted the principal sacred and political narratives of the Christian faith. I was frustrated that the

places that inspired religious devotion were so far removed from my own experience.

"Ustaniji, why are all these religious places so far away?" I asked.

She smiled, for my question provided her an opportunity to explain that the mystical practices that were so central to her faith were inherently and essentially local. She taught me that one should always pray to Allah, but that one could also go to a shrine or *dargah* and offer *fatiha* (prayers) for the saint buried there. I was pleased when she told me that Sindh, the Pakistani state in which I lived, had one of the highest concentrations of Sufi shrines anywhere in the world.

At age ten, however, I didn't quite understand what all this meant.

"Who are the Sufis?" I asked.

"The Sufis are unusual human beings who have given themselves to the service of mankind in the name of Allah," Ustaniji replied. "By submitting one's will to God one can find great satisfaction by achieving the experience of union with the Divine in this life." She added, "There are many Sufis in our part of the world and each has something unique to teach us."

Ustaniji told me that different saints approached their message from different premises. Each experienced his own moment of comprehension, and each communicated to his disciples his unique message of divine love. Sufis were God-lovers and God-seekers, some were stern patriarchs, and others were ecstatic vagabonds. They were scholars, musicians, composers, farmers, and tradesmen, even dancers and poets—they came from all walks of life. Some engaged in the more mundane occupation of politics, bringing their belief in love and tolerance to the practice of statecraft. Many of them believed in reinforcing the better self through discipline and hard work. These mystical leaders, wanderers, and teachers contributed to the spread of Islam in the Indian subcontinent.

In another lesson we discussed one of the most influential early Sufi thinkers. Muhyiuddin ibn al-Arabi (d. CE 1240; AH 637), known in the Sufi tradition as al-Shaikh al-Akbar or Ibn Arabi, was born in CE 1165 (AH 560) in Murcia, Spain, and was initiated into Sufism at the age of twenty. He then spent three decades of travel as a wandering scholar, poet, and mystic, visiting the areas known today as the Maghreb, Egypt, Arabia, Syria, and Asia Minor before settling in Damascus in CE 1223 (AH 619). His philosophical system—*wahdat al-wujud,* his theory of the Unity of Being— incorporates ideas drawn from Greco-Gnostic, Christian, Persian, Islamic, and Jewish thought. Unity of Being, propounded most systematically in his treatises *Insha al-Dawahir* and *Fusus al-Hikam*, exerted an enormous influence among Muslims across the world and had a lasting impact on the Sufi tradition in South Asia. Its basic tenets—that Being is One, that this Being is God (Allah), that everything else is His manifestation, and that, therefore, the world is identical with God—represents a central belief of Islamic mysticism in South Asia.

The doctrine of *wahdat al-wujud* is also inextricably linked to Ibn Arabi's theory of the purpose of creation: the yearning on the part of God to know Himself. This idea is best captured in Ibn Arabi's saying from *hadith qudsi* (prophetic traditions): "I was a hidden treasure, and I loved to be known; so I created the world that I might be known."[1] Moreover, according to Ibn Arabi, from the yearning to know God emerges the human yearning for self-perfection. This perfection consists of the expression of one's own self through the temporal and eternal qualities that manifest themselves in the world process.

"We are fortunate to have such spiritual riches," Ustaniji told me. "Many of the Muslim mystics in this region are inspired by Ibn Arabi's teachings. Remember this lesson when you travel: Take the best from each place and sow the idea in a new place. That is how knowledge multiplies. We can all carry the message of peace and love and understanding. We will visit a Sufi shrine and you will feel the power of the shaikh's spirit. It is these people who give the poor succor. At their shrines there is no distinction between rich and poor; all are welcome and all are equal before Allah. There are mosques built within their complexes to honor Allah. These places are abodes of peace. One day you will go to Ajmer, too. You will see."

And I was desperate to see. The mosques that I visited with my family, like mosques the world over, were places of worship, built so that the faithful could gather together and concentrate their minds on the contemplation of the Divine. God, after all, was everywhere: "To Allah belongs the East and the West. Wherever you turn, there is the presence of God," it states in the Qur'an Baqara (2:115). Through Ustaniji's stories, a new dimension of Islam was emerging for me, and the prospect that physical places existed where the life of the spirit could be nurtured fired my spiritual curiosity. I could not wait to experience these *dargahs*, or "abodes of peace." Perhaps they would help me navigate the religious complexity that both enriched and confounded my relationship to Islam.

When Ustaniji came in the afternoon, I asked her to tell me more about the special prayers and the mystical powers found at a Sufi shrine. I was keen to know how they worked. She said that people who are devoted

89

to a Sufi saint come from near and far to experience the atmosphere of the shrine. The spiritual essence—called *baraka,* or "grace"—can be felt when one visits a saint's resting place.

I know now from experience that these sacred places are symbols for people to make sense of their lives. These spiritual centers attract pilgrims who hope to have a direct experience of the sacred, invisible, supernatural order either in the material aspect of healing or in the immaterial aspect of the inward transformation of the spirit. They function as sites for visitation, prayer, intercession, and music. During my visits I have felt the power that infuses the surrounding areas with historical and spiritual significance. These sites trace the historical cross-pollination between Arabic, Persian, Turkish, Central Asian, and Indian traditions. So many travelers and pilgrims have come and preached and sung there that these sacred gathering places have become centers of diverse points of view. Even today, this diversity thrives, and some two-thirds of the population of South Asia has some allegiance to a shrine.

Requesting that a wish be granted is a ritual common at all Sufi shrines, and I asked Ustaniji to tell me more about these prayers for intercession. She told me that if the prayer to a saint is to be answered, it must come with a vow to be fulfilled. People who visit the shrine address Allah, the Prophet, and the saint, and make a vow in combination with a plea to fulfill a personal need or wish. This wish and vow is called a *mannat.* Devotees believe that prayers offered at the shrine are guided by the spiritual master whose tomb it is.

Ustaniji said that the most famous example of a *mannat* is a well-known story about the Mughal emperor Akbar, who ruled from CE 1556 to 1605 (AH 963–1013). To unite the people of his Indian empire, Akbar advocated the fusion of mystical Islam, or Sufism, with the indigenous practices of the subcontinent. A devotee of Shaikh Salim Chishti, Akbar called his syncretic philosophy the *Din-i-Ilahi* ("Belief in the Divine"). Akbar followed an eclectic personal set of beliefs and practices, set within a basic Islamic framework. He encouraged everyone else similarly, to believe and practice whatever allowed them to live and let live: this was his policy of *sulh-i-kull* meaning "peace with all" or "universal peace"—very Sufi in flavor and origin. The Din-i-Ilahi itself was a private cult centered around Akbar: he was spiritual master (modeled on a Sufi shaikh) to a select group of nobles who swore unquestioning allegiance to him as disciples, and were in fact expected to behave like bound *murids*—like Arthur and his Knights of the Round Table, or Christ and his Apostles.

Shaikh Salim Chishti (CE 1479–1572; AH 883–979) was a Sufi mystic who lived in the village of Sikri near Agra. The prayers of this spiritual master are said to have cured the sick, answered needs, and fulfilled many a thwarted desire. The Emperor Akbar went to Sikri to seek him out. He asked Salim to pray for him that he might be granted a male heir. Akbar's vow was that should his *mannat* be granted he would establish his capital near the abode of the mystic. One year later his prayers were answered with the birth of Salim, who ruled as emperor under the name Jahangir. Akbar's gratitude for the divine favor prompted him to found a city on the spot where his prayers were answered, and Fatehpur Sikri became the primary royal residence. So began several decades of Sufi influence on the Mughal dynasty. After Shaikh Salim Chishti died, Akbar had a tomb erected above the site of his original *khanqah*. Built in CE 1580 and 1581 (AH 987–988), the mausoleum is considered one of the finest examples of Mughal architecture in India.

After hearing such stories of *mannats*, I confessed to Ustaniji that I had a secret wish I wanted Allah to grant. More than anything, I wanted something that I knew was nearly impossible: to study in America. Fearful of telling anyone my wish, I prayed every day, hoping that this extra bit of effort might allow my prayers to reach heaven faster. Ustaniji had told me that at the shrine we would say our prayers as usual, and that after reciting the last three *sura*s (chapters) of the Qur'an I could make a *mannat*. Some women tie a piece of thread or a strip of cloth to the lattice around the tomb or on the branches of a tree in the courtyard as a reminder of their wish and vow. Once the wish has been granted and the vow fulfilled, it is customary to visit the shrine again, offer a prayer of thanks, and remove the thread or cloth. This completes the circle of prayer.

When I learned that shrines held spiritual powers different from those in our own home, which until now had been the center of my universe, I begged my parents to arrange a trip to a shrine. After many entreaties, my mother finally agreed to take us to the town of Bhit Shah in Sindh, a day's journey from Karachi. We prepared for this journey with great excitement. Ustaniji told us that Bhit Shah was the burial place of Shah Abdul Latif Bhittai (CE 1689–1752; AH 1100–1165), who was known among the Sindhis as Shah (or "monarch") because he was the greatest Sindhi poet. People pay their respects to Shah Abdul Latif because they consider him to be a friend of God—a saint and guide to the spiritual and material turmoil of life on earth. His shrine was built by his followers to commemorate his teachings and his extraordinary contribution to poetry, in which he seeks to explain the relationship between man and God.

We set off on the road to Thatta in two cars: one filled to capacity with Ustaniji, three of my younger brothers, my sister and myself, and hampers of food; a second one with my mother, the two other wives of my father, and our servant Majid. My father was too busy to accompany us, so he sent us off under the care of Majid and our drivers, one of whom came from Hala, a town near Bhit Shah, and who felt honored to show us and tell us about his home area. This driver had promised to take us to Jilwagah-i-Imamain, a place on Makli Hill where the Prophet is supposed to have appeared to the faithful.

As we sped north, our driver told us that his favorite poet, Mir Ali Sher Qani, sings a song about the Jilwagah-i-Imamain:

> It is paradise on earth, full of hope,
> It is the visiting place of men of God.
> It is not a star that shines in that place—
> An angel's eye was opened for the sake of looking …
> You do not see on its sky the new moon—
> Rather, it is the eyebrow on the eyes of angels …[2]

I imagined the night sky full of stars that were angels looking down at us. The universe seemed full of possibilities.

When our cars finally pulled into Thatta, we stopped to wash and refresh ourselves at an old rest house at Makli Hill. Out of the car at last, we set off with Ustaniji to explore. I felt what I had heard about through so many stories: Makli is infused with a spiritual atmosphere emanating from tombs belonging to royalty and military commanders, saints and scholars, philosophers and poets. The place feels inhabited by spirits and exerts a mysterious attraction. This same feeling was obviously apparent to local rulers of successive generations who would erect their own tombs near the tombs of Sufi masters to benefit from the power of prayers offered by visiting pilgrims to the nearby saints. I could imagine the ghost of Alexander the Great, who rested his weary troops near here before his almost-fatal march across the Makran Desert in Balochistan. Squinting my eyes to avoid the sun, I could see Alexander's Admiral Niarchos readying the fleet for the voyage along the coast of the Arabian Sea. I could imagine the legendary Mughal emperor Shah Jahan, builder of the Taj Mahal, who passed through here in the seventeenth century and ordered the construction of the great Mosque of Thatta. As we walked toward the burial place of Jam Nizamuddin, the Samma Rajput Muslim leader and patron of the arts whose tomb bore motifs from the catalog of Hindu decorations, a *faqir*, an ascetic wanderer wearing a long black robe and

bright orange turban, sat on the desert sand surrounded by desert shrubs and sang the folk ballad of Sassi wandering in the desert looking for her beloved Punnun. Stories were everywhere.

Tired from clambering about Makli Hill, we sought the refuge of the rest house, where we busied ourselves with eating food the cook had packed for us—kebabs and *rotis*, cool slices of melon, carrots and apples, and hard-boiled eggs wrapped in waxed paper with little packets of salt and pepper. When my mother saw a fellow traveler in the rest house, she invited him to share our meal. While I habitually thanked Allah and my family for providing so well for me before every meal, my gratitude took on a new meaning given the nature of our journey. Gratitude and charity, I realized, were part of a complex system of rights, duties, and responsibilities related to our membership in a spiritual community. Sharing food with those less fortunate was not merely kindness on my mother's part, but was also considered part of her responsibility as a Muslim.

Resuming our journey after lunch, we crossed a bridge over the river Indus on the outskirts of Hyderabad and approached the small town of Hala, the last village on the way to Bhit Shah. Our driver was proud to show us the many small ceramic factories where beautiful tiles were still being made to adorn buildings. I was giddy with anticipation. Once just a simple mud village, Bhit Shah had been breathtakingly embellished by the Shah's followers over the years. I could see from a distance its sparkling white domes and glittering blue and white tiles, dancing in the desert sun like a mirage, promising sanctuary and rest.

When we arrived at last within the courtyard of the shrine, I saw the marble cenotaph surrounded by a marble lattice to which countless ribbons—the markers of wishes—were tied. Other more specific wishes had their own special symbolic objects. Votive candles symbolized a mother's wish for fertility. Cowbells expressed the wish to find lost cattle. Other blessings requested in person are written on paper and tied up with a piece of cloth into a woman's veil or a man's turban. Ustaniji explained the significance of each of these we passed, before I even had a chance to ask her.

The mass of pilgrims approaching the shrine became a throng of uniform movement. I found myself in lockstep with an elderly woman. The deep lines in her face clearly held many stories.

"*Maasi*," I asked in my broken Sindhi—the local language in which some of the servants and vendors in my Karachi neighborhood conversed— "Have you come here to make a wish too?"

93

She explained that she wanted to get an amulet for her disabled son from the shrine's keepers. She introduced me to her son, and it appeared to me that he must have had polio as a child. The woman believed absolutely in the positive effect the amulet would have. While the shrine's *faqirs* continued their chants, the keepers of the shrine dispensed tokens of the shrine's mystical powers, and the woman pointed to where they sat, behind a curtain toward the back of the shrine. She would go to them to make her request. She was also waiting for an audience with the *sajjada-nashin*—Shah Abdul Latif's descendant, who, she believed, had the power to dispense blessings. I was overwhelmed. I pulled at the hem of Ustaniji's sari. "Is it time to ask the saint for my wish?"

She looked at me intently. "Yes, my child, but you must not make such a wish by praying to human beings, living or dead—only to God. Veneration of those with great spiritual power can never substitute for devotion to God. While you are here at the shrine, you can declare your wish and desire for guidance and we will tie this ribbon on the lattice as a symbol. Remember, the saint is only an intercessor, as his learning has brought him nearer to God than you."

As if on cue, the muezzin issued his call to prayer, the *azan*, at exactly that moment, reminding me of where my prayers were to be directed.

Allah u Akbar, Allah u Akbar …
Allah is Great, Allah is Great …

The muezzin finished his call, and we all began to offer our prayers. Shrines such as these always have mosques attached, but unlike more formal mosques, here there was no physical segregation of genders. The convention is that women tend to congregate on one side of the courtyard and men on the other, but the design of the shrine did not mandate it. In the act of praying together, the relationship to God is personal but also collective and spread among all the faithful at the same time worldwide. The profound fellowship with my Muslim brothers and sisters resonated more powerfully with me in this special place where worship referred to an inclusive and integrated body of believers comprising thousands of active participants.

As always, the repetitive action and recitation of prayer focused my mind. Clear-headed, I felt ready to make my wish. I walked up to the lattice and tied the string I had brought from home. I closed my eyes and thanked God for the women in my life who stood next to me, my mother and Ustaniji, who had nurtured me and encouraged me to dream. What I wanted most in the world was to study in America. I wished that I would travel throughout the world and learn. I asked Allah to grant my wish if He in His wisdom thought it was in my best interest.

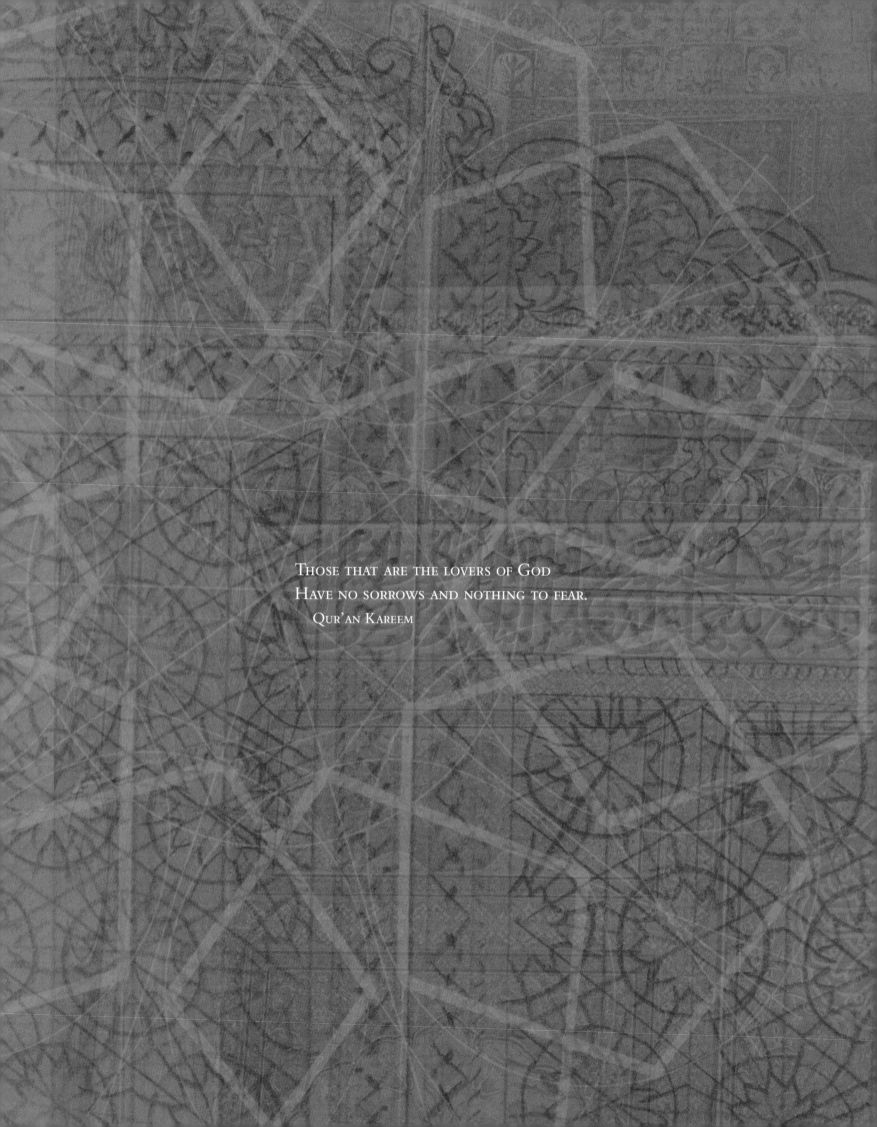

THOSE THAT ARE THE LOVERS OF GOD
HAVE NO SORROWS AND NOTHING TO FEAR.

QUR'AN KAREEM

ترجمہ: جو اللہ کے ولی ہوتے ہیں انہیں کوئی خوف یا غم نہ ہوگا۔ (قرآن کریم)

Somewhere near Multan

All roads come from Eternity.

The Bullock carts, and the goats,
sad little donkeys with hanging ears
in the fields, near the thatched huts;
camel, carrying cotton bales, day after day.

From the colourful trucks
blossom the dreams of the poor,
and the reed longs to sign of man's fate.

The nameless heroines of poverty,
lifting their pitchers, await
the water of life.

All roads point to Eternity.

And their centre rests
under the sky-like dome
in the heart of the saint.

  Annemarie Schimmel

Bhit Shah
Shah Abdul Latif,
a *Mannat* Fulfilled

Lahore
Data Ganj Bakhsh Hujwiri,
Patron Saint of the Indus

Ajmer
Khwaja Muinuddin Hasan Chishti,
Keeper of the Poor

Delhi
Nizamuddin Auliya and
the Faqir Princess Jahanara

Lahore
Mian Mir and
the Unity of Existence

Multan
Shaikh Rukn-i-Alam,
the Pillar of the World

Lahore
Madho Lal Husain
and the Festival of Lamps

Kasur
The Mystical Poetry of
Bulleh Shah

If the secret of the sound you know, the Echo and the Call are the same. They both were one; in hearing alone they became two. One palace, lakhs of doors, and millions of windows—wherever I look I behold the Lord face to face.

Shah Abdul Latif

Shah Abdul Latif,
a Mannat Fulfilled

Decades later, I returned to the shrine of Shah Abdul Latif with a friend. The *mannat* I had made on that first trip to Bhit Shah with Ustaniji had been fulfilled. I had been given the gift of education. I had traveled the world. Now, as the climate in the world had become filled with tensions and unease, questions kept rising in my heart and mind.

But my desire to return to Bhit Shah in adulthood was more than a debt of gratitude, and the spiritual resonance of the shrine was not exclusively retrospective. My studies in the United States had introduced me to Professor Annemarie Schimmel, one of the greatest scholars of Islamic mystical tradition. Prof. Schimmel encouraged me to explore the Sufi tradition, just as Ustaniji had done in my childhood. When she saw the books I had made, she said that the work I was meant for was to build a bridge between my culture and others. I asked her to explain. In response she told me the story of Sassi and Punnun. I had grown up listening to this story on the rooftop of my family home, but it wasn't until my education with Prof. Schimmel began that I came to understand this tale, and others like it, as a Sufi parable, infused with the allegories of the soul's reunification with the Divine. The tales had always led me to meditate on the many variations of this journey, expressed as a search for the lost beloved in one's heart. Prof. Schimmel reminded me that while the *hajj* (pilgrimage to Mecca) is one of the Pillars of Islam, pilgrimage to saints' tombs is also a feature of piety. Sindh was a sacred place for her, and she often said she wanted to be buried there. Her reading of the Sassi and Punnun legend stayed with me as I again crossed the desert of Sindh, past Hyderabad and Bhambore and Thatta, retracing the steps of my earlier journey.

SAMINA QURAESHI

A mere forty miles from Karachi lies Bambhore, the entry point
of the Arab Muhammad bin Qasim into Sindh in the eighth century.
Ruins of a mosque at Bambhore testify to the earliest sign of a permanent
Muslim settlement in South Asia, with an engraved Kufic inscription that
memorializes Muhammad bin Qasim's introduction of Islam into Sindh.
Though little remains of the town, save for some bricks and flat earthen
tiles, extant traces evoke the once magnificent civilization on the banks
of the river Indus. From this port, Sindh became a relay point from which
the highly developed mathematical and scientific innovations of India were
transmitted to the Arabic centers of learning in the Middle East. But at age
ten, when I first ventured into Sindh, Bambhore was most significant to me
as the locus of the famous folk legend of Sassi and Punnun.

Sassi was the adopted daughter of a washerman. Tales of her beauty
attracted Punnun, the prince of Kech in Balochistan, who fell so in love
with her that he abandoned his title and his people to stay in Bambhore.
One night his treacherous relatives stole into Bambhore and kidnapped
him. Sassi, bereft, followed the caravan to Kech on foot. She perished
in the desert calling for her beloved. Their tragic tale of impossible love
reads alternately as a cautionary tale warning against love outside one's
community or as a Sufi parable of the soul's longing for reunification with
the Divine Beloved. But in both cases, it is a tale of courage and ardor that
asserts the primacy of love in human experience, whether tellers of the tale
consider Sassi and Punnun as irrational dreamers too immature to see the
wisdom of sticking to one's own kind or as spiritual seekers convinced that
the eternal is immanent in romantic love. The popularity of the tale attests
to the universality of myth, drawing comparisons with Romeo and Juliet,
Pyramus and Thisbe, or Majnun and Laila, but also points to the role of oral
tradition and allegory in sustaining the cultural memory of the region.

Tales such as this form a crucial point of departure for Shah Abdul
Latif's *Risalo*, or poetic treatise. The Shah's *Risalo* is divided into thirty *surs*
(song chapters) that retell the stories and legends of the Indus and give the
female voice to his protagonists. Shah Abdul Latif made the ideas of the
great Sufi spiritual master and poet Maulana Jalaluddin Rumi (CE 1207–
1273; AH 603–671) and classical Sufi literature relevant to the daily lives
of illiterate villagers of Sindh, giving them the feeling that they, too, had
access to Divine truth.

Until Shah Abdul Latif started composing verses in Sindhi, most Sufis,
including Rumi, wrote in Persian. Shah Adul Latif's most popular work,
the story of Sassi and Punnun, describes the spiritual journey of his heroine,
who remained faithful to the Divine Beloved, and his verses reflect the
landscape and essential qualities of Sindh: images of thorn trees, the tidal

106

Sassi in the Desert

I walk

and the blood of my feet

　　transforms the stones into roses.

I walk

and the tears of my eyes

　　water the desert shrubs,

Every day the same sun,

　　scorching, merciless white,

And at nightfall the wind cutting my heart and hope.

I walk out of myself.

And the desert is you.

The paths are throbbing like veins,

and tenderly touches my hand

your skin, soft as sand.

I wander through you,

drinking the salty water that flows from your eyes,

sleeping at night in your arms

when you cover my weary limbs

with your garment of stars.

　　And I am

one with the beats of your heart,

one with your breath, with the wind.[3]

Annemarie Schimmel

swirls of the Indus, the characteristic thatched huts. His vivid descriptions of harsh conditions of the desert and the merciful bounty of rain gave the local population a poignant and comprehensible parable of God's grace. Through the use of local folk tales, Shah Abdul Latif's poetry elaborates the soul's movements: hope, longing, fear, annihilation, and finally union: these are the stages of the "interior journey" toward the Divine. The use of folk legends was a well-established tradition in religious teaching in the region, and Sufi teachers tapped it since their congregants were familiar with these tragic tales and could identify with the universal sentiments and the local customs and geography that they referred to.

On my return to Bhit Shah, I was struck by the growing throng of merchants and pilgrims as we came closer to the entrance of the shrine. I remembered the wish I had asked to be granted and my secret vow so many years ago, when I had asked God, with Ustaniji at my side and Shah Abdul Latif as interlocutor, to give me the strength and the opportunity to study in America. I also remembered, just before I tied the string to the lattice, that I asked my mother, "How many cousins do I have?" Preoccupied, she brushed me off with the answer, "one hundred." I multiplied this seemingly incalculable sum by three and vowed to return to feed three hundred hungry pilgrims.

In the bazaar surrounding the shrine there were flower markets, garlands of money and flowers, scribes writing letters and contracts, teachers giving various kinds of instruction, people selling replicas of the shrine in clay and marble, food stalls, sweetmeats, milky tea, and icy drinks. It was so thick with pilgrims that we had to get out of the car on the outskirts of the village. As we walked toward the entrance to the shrine past ever-increasing hives of activity, I quickly noticed that almost no one else had arrived by car. Villagers from the surrounding area, wearing colorful Sindhi costumes, arrived by camel or horse cart. Pilgrims from farther afield traveled on highly decorated local buses. We were in a different world from the sophisticated and cosmopolitan Karachi that I was used to.

I was aware that such a sense of community uniting people across usually rigid socioeconomic and ethnic divides was exceptionally rare in the context of Pakistan's extreme social stratification. Our mosque in Karachi was open to everyone, but the city's spatial segregation meant that congregants were more likely to be from our neighborhood, which meant families of means and the people who worked for them. In Bhit Shah, such distinctions evaporated in the teeming sea of pilgrims. The promenade to the shrine of the saint was littered with stalls selling everything from a fluffy white *mithai* made from milk to cloth sheets printed with the *kalima*—the primary prayer that there is no God but God—to drape over the tomb as a mark of respect. Food vendors cheerfully dispensed tea and snacks to the faithful as they made their way to the shrine. The final steps along the path led past flower stalls with baskets of rose petals and garlands of blossoms. Pilgrims buy these garlands to place on the tombs of the Shah and his followers as a symbol of the fragrance of the Lord that surrounds their final resting place.

As I passed through the entrance to the shrine itself I was surprised by its tranquility. The *qawwali* had not yet started, and things were relatively quiet around the shrine. I approached the custodians, representatives of Shah Abdul Latif, who were assembled at the entrance to the cenotaph. I had to speak to them to fulfill the oath portion of my *mannat*.

Custodians such as these often belonged to the family of the Sufi shaikh. In the absence of a property-owning aristocracy, many *sajjadas*, heirs to the shaikh, and *makhdums*, descendants of the shaikh, assumed a status not entirely dissimilar to that enjoyed by feudal lords in other societies. Because the shrine sits on tax-free land and the land passes on to the shaikh's heirs, offerings made there are tied to the land but enjoyed by the *makhdums* as substantial sources of personal wealth. The belief of unlettered people in the powers of a shaikh made them loyal followers of the shaikh's "successor" and useful for political purposes. The inheritance of the *makhdums* from their saintly ancestors was thus personal wealth and political power, with their corollary of a capacity for oppression. In the social anarchy of Mughal decline in the mid-nineteenth century, in the vacuum of royal decay and aristocratic ineptitude, the *makhdums* and *sajjadas* gained immense influence, particularly in Sindh and southern Punjab. Many of these descendants bear little resemblance philosophically to their saintly forebears, but all demand respect, money, offerings of livestock, and lifelong service from the peasantry. There are instances of this power being used for benign or humanitarian purposes, but these are exceptional. This contradiction to the original message of the Sufis and their embrace of poverty and simplicity is a troubling symptom of the social inequities that persist in these lands.

At the time the Sufi saints Shah Abdul Latif and Baba Farid were preaching they wielded enormous temporal power over their followers, who were mostly from the surrounding areas. Baba Farid himself, for instance, functioned much like a medieval European feudal lord. What has changed in modern times is the balance between power and responsibility—in a functional feudal system the lord is bound by responsibilities as great as his powers. Someone like Baba Farid would have held his power by virtue of his personal charisma and active contribution to the community as a healer, arbiter, advisor, spiritual protector, and regulatory authority. Like the

European feudal manor, the *dargah* (shrine) traditionally functioned as the seat of government for the lands constituting its *waqf* (endowment). What happened to the *makhdums* and *sajjada-nashins* is what sometimes happened to the Indian princes under colonial rule: landowners who were confirmed and legalized under the colonial dispensation tended to become corrupt and despotic because the all-powerful and all-regulating colonial state now stood as the guarantor of their power and wealth—thereby stripping them of the social responsibilities that their position had traditionally rested on.

Today, the peasants of Sindh, repressed by landlords and mired in poverty, have much to escape from. The shrines of the saints give refuge and provide food, and the *qawwali* allows pilgrims to vent their frustration and achieve temporary respite from despair. For the ill, the sad, and the lonely, shrines are often the only recourse available. As I observed the conditions of so many of the pilgrims, I was aware not only of the economic desperation of the local population, but also of their deep spiritual devotion.

I approached the custodians to have them accept my offering. "I want to fulfill my *mannat*," I said.

"And what is your *mannat*?" one of them asked.

"To feed three hundred, should I be given the grace of education."

Sitting before a desk on the floor, the *makhdum* spoke to me of the spiritual meaning and rewards of charity as he wrote talismans and Qur'anic verses as blessings. I heard echoes of Ustaniji in this man's words and so I told him her story. He told me I was lucky to have had access to one so wise in my personal spiritual development. Tears filled my eyes as I recounted that my great fortune in spiritual mentors had not stopped with Ustaniji. My educational journey had introduced me to another wise soul, my Apaji, Annemarie Schimmel. She and I had spent countless hours discussing her scholarly interpretations of the same devotional practices that Ustaniji knew and taught me from memory. Prof. Schimmel had given me important lessons in these traditions and reminded me once again of the vital role of women in the course of my own spiritual development. I made a new vow to search for other women who were religious teachers in the diversity of religious practice and interpretation within Islam.

The *makhdums* were very interested in my story. The learned eyes of one in particular, older than the rest, brightened at the mention of Annemarie Schimmel's name. "She is a great teacher. She understands better than most the complexity of the Divine Beloved." He went on, "My child, I hope you understand that this is not a debt. This is just one part of

refining your own search for the divine qualities that are hidden in your soul, such as charity. Each one of us carries the divine within."

Indeed, I thought, sacred space is within one's soul. I realized that access to that space was made possible through prayer and meditation. I had learned that I must begin each day by saying to God, "I am doing my very best. Please help me by showing me the way." And I was comforted to think that such vows are not bargaining for blessings, but in fact honoring the principle of charity that is an integral part of my understanding of the guidance of the *hadith*.

In my return to this sanctuary, I saw again the local expressions of exuberant piety. The cultural impact of learned Sufis is a living tradition. The power of these places emanates from the fact that there is nothing static about devotion. While all of our prayers are directed toward Allah alone and pay homage to the life and work of the Prophet Muhammad, the evolution of true piety is not frozen in the seventh century. It breathes with each prayer of the faithful over time, and in specific places.

The caretakers often recited the story of Shah Abdul Latif, who was born in Hala, near present-day Hyderabad in Sindh in CE 1689 (AH 1100). Latif's great-great-grandfather was a well-known mystic poet by the name of Abdul Karim Shah. Shah Abdul Latif's father, Shah Habib, was revered by many as a pious man. Shah Habib had sought the blessings of many holy men. One dervish blessed him with the birth of a son and said that he would become the *qutb*, the pole star of his times. Shah Abdul Latif's mother was a descendant of another mystic, Makhdum Dayani, known as *majzub*—"divinely intoxicated."

People from far and wide came to Shah Habib to acquire his blessings, and poets in particular came to gain his advice and instruction in the art of poetics. Shah Habib advocated using Sindhi as the language for poetry rather than courtly Persian, for he believed that a poet could best express himself in his native language. Shah Habib's household was a gathering place for poets and intellectuals, and into this environment Shah Abdul Latif was born.

During his youth Shah Abdul Latif learned Arabic, Persian, Hindi, and Sindhi. There are many stories that reveal Latif's mystical devotion even as a child. He was placed under the care of a tutor who started by teaching him the alphabet. The tutor asked Latif to say "*alif*," the first letter of the alphabet, which represents the word *Allah* (God). Latif repeated it. The tutor then asked him to say "*ba*," the second letter. Latif refused, insisting that there was no "*ba*." The tutor wondered at this stubbornness and told Latif's father, who, being a wise man himself, understood that the child was making a statement about the oneness of God and the fact that all things began and ended with Him. Latif continued his education. It is said that the Qur'an in Arabic, Rumi's *Masnawi* in Persian, and his great-great-grandfather Shah Abdul Karim's *bait*s (couplets) in Sindhi were Latif's constant companions. He was enamored of the poetry and ideas of the great Sufi poet Shah Inayat and his quest for justice for landless peasants. As a young man he traveled with the yogis and *faqirs* of Sindh. Impressed by their spirituality, he reflected what he heard in his own poems. Many Hindu scholars of Sindh revere Shah Abdul Latif's work as an expression of Hindu mysticism. Many Hindus continue to visit his shrine. For them, Latif's work expresses the interaction of the two faiths, and despite the fundamentalists' dictums against it, this syncretism survives.

During Latif's lifetime his popularity with the local people and his association with Shah Inayat made many powerful landlords suspicious, and they opposed his teachings. Over time, however, even the landlords became convinced that his verses advocated peace and harmony and posed no threat. Latif sought a place where, in solitude, he could devote all his time to prayer and meditation. He found that the hills near Lake Karar, not far from his birthplace of Hala, possessed the harsh and untamed beauty of the desert. He eventually settled here at a place called Bhit–a "sand hill" covered by small, thorny *kikar* trees and surrounded by many pools of water. Here he collected his disciples around him, and after a while the makeshift camp was replaced by simple dwellings of mud and brick. Over the centuries, Shah Latif's mausoleum has been enlarged and embellished by his devotees and now appears to hover majestically above the surrounding land. It looks like a mirage in the hazy heat. The shimmering image of thin minarets and cupolas reaching to the sky makes it look and feel like an oasis, like water in the middle of this parched desert, an island adorned with lotus flowers to remind pilgrims of the lake that once was there.

Shah Abdul Latif's shrine is home to a band of *faqirs*—mendicants and ascetics who have renounced the world to dedicate themselves to learning the music that he created to heal the spirit. The *faqirs* sing accompanied by the *tamboro*, a musical instrument the shaikh invented, every day of the year from sunset to dawn. The music they perform is known as the *Shah jo Rag*, intricate pieces sung in a haunting falsetto that are said to have curative powers. People from all over bring the sick and the troubled to spend the night absorbing the prayers and the chants, constantly repeating the name of God. The *faqirs*, who are accomplished musicians and performers of the poet's compositions, live in the shrine complex.

Grounded in the experiences of rural Sindh, Shah Abdul Latif's poems are said to be the "crowning achievement" of the Sindhi language. At the

same time, the Shah's poetry has a timeless appeal for ordinary people, reflecting their trials and triumphs, and suggesting that suffering is only temporary and that the individual can attain salvation by trying to return to his divine essence. Sindhis from all walks of life look to his poetry for inspiration and wisdom. Shah Latif teaches his devotees about the universal equality of the human race: about the dignity of labor, peace for humanity, the performance of good and virtuous actions, religious tolerance, hard work, and union with the eternal truth through humility and humanity.

Music was a language for Latif, and during his lifetime musicians were always present at Bhit to perform for him. He composed his poetry using classical Indian scales (*ragas*), and his music and verse were designed to accompany and complement each other. It is said that at the time of his death, Shah Abdul Latif remained in a solitary chamber for twenty days. On the twenty-first day he emerged to take a bath. He then returned and asked those present to play music and sing songs as he lay down and pulled a sheet over his head. For three days the musicians sang and played until he passed away.

We visited Bhit Shah during the *urs*, which marks the Shah's death anniversary with pilgrimage, singing and music, and a literary festival that celebrates his life as a poet. On the occasion of the *urs*, the *sajjada* (whose family and followers—*murids*—live near the shrine complex) dons the cap and cloak of Shah Abdul Latif and leads the procession to the shrine accompanied by weeping and chanting devotees. Everywhere I turned, I saw, heard, or smelled another ritual act: the lighting of oil lamps, recitations of the Qur'an, singing of Latif's *Risalo*, the placing of new *chadars*, or sheets, on the tomb. My senses were overpowered with the distinctive scents of myrrh and sandalwood incense and garlands of jasmine and roses.

Keepers of the shrine circulated throughout the courtyard, offering water and asking if people needed anything. Three times a day, the cooks among them prepared and offered a simple *biryani*, a delicious layered dish of meat, rice, and potatoes. The preparation of food such as this presents an opportunity for visitors to contribute monetarily to the upkeep of the shrine and its many functions. Sharing food with those less fortunate and paying *zakat*—a percentage of one's income given as alms for the poor—is one of the Five Pillars of Islam. I made my contribution by arranging to feed three hundred pilgrims as I had promised in the making of my *mannat*, so many years ago.

At night the shrine is lit up in multicolored fairy lights and packed with people. Inside, men draped in the traditional *ajrak*, a textile printed in

crimson and indigo, sway and sing verses of the saint's poems, while women and children light sandalwood and rose incense before they place their belongings on the floor and embark upon the night's ecstatic homage and remembrance. They settle down to listen to the *Shah jo Rag*, an incantatory form of worship through music. As I listened to the unrelenting and rhythmic repetition of the Shah's lyrical poetry, I felt that he was talking directly to me, that he was present, calling out to all his devotees. I saw a woman who had appeared old and feeble arise and begin to twirl, dancing the *dhamal*, swinging her body to the beat of the drums, calling on God to bless her so that her prayer would be granted. A newly married couple I had noticed earlier arriving by car, the bride still wearing the bright silk clothes of her trousseau, were also moved to sing; for all their finery and urban sophistication, they closed their eyes and swayed.

> If the secret of the sound you know, the Echo and the Call are the
> same. They both were one; in hearing alone they became two.
> One palace, *lakhs* of doors, and millions of windows—wherever I
> look I behold the Lord face to face.[4]

The invocation of Shah Abdul Latif's words and voice does not express grief at his passing, because the spirit of the holy man is considered eternally present. As we sat at night in the courtyard of the shrine, my friend—who was not given to such mystical notions—acknowledged that something powerful was emanating from the shaikh's resting place. Perhaps the cumulative effect of so many prayers and wishes in such intense concentration over so many years is what makes the place feel so spiritually charged. Thinking of the intractable problems that confront us, the terrorism motivated by religion and intolerance that is engulfing my country of Pakistan, I looked for a moment of inspiration. I sought a way to communicate this transcendent experience, to lift those proponents of violence beyond the intolerance in which they are mired. I closed my eyes, and prayed for peace.

The Melody of the Dawn

Of wandering minstrels this is not the custom

With idle musical instrument their shoulders to accustom.

You have ceased to admire the beautiful dawn,

With it you are now at daggers drawn.

Who will you a devoted minstrel call,

If your instrument does not music play at all?

So late how can you keep asleep?

Awake! It is the dawn! Weep! Weep!

Your instrument on the morrow's advent

Will be in the dust and for ever lament!

The instrument under your head you kept,

And from dusk to dawn you slept.

How can you, a minstrel, thus become

An honoured one in the world to come?

Of those whom minstrels you name,

Who believe to relax is a shame,

Their instrument they carry on their shoulder,

Seek their Path, and in the desert wander.

Shah Abdul Latif

فَاذْكُرُونِي أَذْكُرْكُمْ

Then do ye remember Me; I will remember you.

Qur'an 2:152

In this age, however, God has veiled
most people from Sufism and
from its votaries, and has concealed
its mysteries from their hearts.

   Hujwiri

Data Ganj Bakhsh Hujwiri, Patron Saint of the Indus

Leaving Karachi and traveling up the Indus I encountered many other stories. The country I passed through changed from desert to farmland as I neared southern Punjab. I was headed for Pakpattan to learn about Baba Farid Shakar Ganj ("the Treasure of Sugar") when I was told that all spiritual journeys in Punjab start in Lahore, where Data Ganj Bakhsh, the patron saint of this region, lies entombed. I asked about Data, and what I learned made me alter course and head for Lahore.

In the eleventh century, Data Ganj Bakhsh, also known as Hujwiri, settled in Lahore after many wanderings. He was a renowned Sufi and one of the earliest and most revered mystical thinkers of his time. His spiritual *silsila*, the "chain" of teaching, connects him to Hazrat Ali, the son-in-law of the Prophet Muhammad. Data's magnum opus, the *Kashf al-Mahjub* ("The Unveiling of the Hidden"), is said to be one of the first Persian treatises on the mystical life, and to this day it remains influential. Hujwiri died in CE 1071 (AH 463), and his tomb became a place of pilgrimage and the spiritual center of the Punjab. It was considered to be the gateway to India for all those mystics from Iran and Central Asia who entered the northwestern plains of the subcontinent. There is a widespread belief that Data had "supreme authority over the saints of India and no new saint entered the country without first obtaining permission from his spirit."[5] Some continued on their way, deeper into what is now India, with the aim of spreading the teachings of the mystical dimensions of Islam: Love of God, Love of the Prophet, and Love of One's Fellow Human Beings.

We traversed the fertile plains of the Punjab, a land named for the five rivers—the Jhelum, Chenab, Ravi, Beas, and Sutlej—that wander through the region as tributaries of the Indus. In the last eleven hundred years the

rivers have seen all religions and ethnicities passing through their lands. On the left bank of the river Ravi we reached the ancient city of Lahore. Legend has it that Lahore was founded by Lav, a son of the Hindu deity Rama. The history of the Old City of Lahore spans thousands of years from its origin as a stopping place for travelers to a seat of the Mughal Empire to the cosmopolitan center of art, culture, and spirituality that it is today.

Leading to the Lahori Gate, one of ten gates into the ancient walled city, is Anarkali Bazaar, a busy, crowded city market with hundreds of shops lining narrow, winding lanes. Rickshaws and donkey carts pick their way through these snug passages. The tightly packed houses loom over the street, and above our heads are carved balconies and pots of colorful bougainvillea. Some of these houses open into courtyards, and it is here and on the rooftops that the Old City conducts its transactions. In the street, there are all sorts of goods. Stalls sell posters of the Sufi shaikhs, commemorative cloths to lay as marks of respect on the shrines, fragrant *pan* leaves to entice areca nut chewers, hair oil, cosmetics, and video cassettes with *qawwali* music and recitations of the Qur'an. The teashops offer tea and a pastrylike *naan* and the chance to gossip with the patrons. Around the southwestern corner of the walled city near the Bhati Gate is a street filled with *degh-wala*s, literally, the "street of cauldrons." Here, food is cooked in enormous pots on charcoal fires and the faithful buy the prepared food to feed the poor who collect daily at the Data Ganj Bakhsh shrine.

Hazrat Sayyad Abul Hasan Makhdum Ali al-Hujwiri was born in Hujwir, Ghazni (in present-day Afghanistan), at the time a hub of intellectual and educational activity, around CE 991 (AH 380). He later came to be known as Data Ganj Bakhsh and Data Sahib. Hujwiri traveled widely, through areas of what are today Egypt, Palestine/Israel, Iran, Iraq, Anatolia, Arabia, Azerbaijan, and Syria. He encountered many Sufi teachers, all of whom influenced the way in which his own ideas took shape. As he traveled and stopped at various shrines, he meditated on spiritual matters, but he also encountered the same sorts of economic concerns that seem to dominate our lives today. Reflecting on his journeys to the territories of Iraq, Hujwiri wrote,[6]

Once, in the territories of 'Iráq, I was restlessly occupied ... in seeking wealth and squandering it, and I had run largely into debt. Everyone who wanted anything turned to me, and I was troubled and at a loss to know how to accomplish their desires. An eminent person wrote to me as follows: "Beware lest you distract your mind from God by satisfying the wishes of those whose minds are engrossed in vanity. If you find anyone whose mind is nobler than

Some regard knowledge as superior to action,

while others put action first, but both are wrong.

Unless action is combined with knowledge,

it is not deserving of recompense.

  Hujwiri

your own, you may justly distract your mind in order to give peace
to his. Otherwise, do not distract yourself since God is sufficient for
His servants.

In the *Kashf al-Mahjub*, Hujwiri recorded his experiences and explored
the relationship between the soul and what God has revealed through
prophetic practice. He situates the Sufi tradition within the framework of
the Qur'an, the *hadith*, and *sharia*, or Islamic sacred law. He insists that a Sufi
must adhere to the outward observances of Islam such as canonical prayers,
or *salat*, and fasting, and that additional practices such as *zikr*, remembrance
of the Divine, can be used to further cultivate the inner dimensions of faith.
His book serves as a Sufi manual of sorts, which presents the teachings of
various Sufi masters and discusses in detail the practices of several different
Sufi orders. Hujwiri saw his work as a tool for the "polishing of hearts
which are bound by the veil of attributes, but in which dwells the Essence
of the Light of Truth." Lamenting the decay of the path of Sufism, Hujwiri
wrote,[7]

> In this age, however, God has veiled most people from Súfiism
> [*sic*] and from its votaries, and has concealed its mysteries from
> their hearts. Accordingly, some imagine that it consists merely
> in the practice of outward piety without inward contemplation,
> and others suppose that it is a form and a system without essence
> and root, to such an extent that they have adopted the view of
> scoffers (*ahl-i hazl*) and theologians (*'ulamá*), who regard only the
> external, and have condemned Súfiism altogether, making no
> attempt to discover what it really is. The people in general, blindly
> conforming to this opinion, have erased from their hearts the quest
> for inward purity and have discarded the tenets of the Ancients and
> the Companions of the Prophet.

The conditions we are living in today, the conflict of modernity with
traditional values, the loss of belief and tolerance and diversity, seem to
reflect what Hujwiri wrote about conditions in his own time. Perhaps such
upheavals come in cycles.

Oral tradition attributes many miraculous occurrences to Hujwiri,
or Data Sahib, adding to his mysterious power. I met a farmer at Sahib's
shrine who told me he was there to ask that his cows produce thick, pure
milk. There was a blight in his village, he explained, that was making his
cows listless and unproductive. I asked him how Data Sahib could help
his cows, since he really dealt with guiding pilgrims to the Divine. He
answered me with a Hujwiri story about the Turkish emirs of Ghazni, who
entered the subcontinent in the eleventh century and made Lahore part

of the Ghaznavid Empire. The governor of Lahore was Rai Raju, a well-known Hindu yogi. The people of Lahore revered him and supplied him with large quantities of milk as homage. Once, a woman carrying a pot of milk passed by Hujwiri. When he asked her if she could give him some, she refused, saying it was meant for Rai Raju. Hujwiri told her that if she gave him some milk, her cow would begin to produce in greater abundance. She complied, and from then on her cow's udders were always full. Soon this news spread all over Lahore and people flocked to Hujwiri, and because of their encounter with him they converted, by the thousands, to Islam.

Rai Raju, curious and infuriated by Hujwiri, sent his emissaries to see what the newcomer was all about. None of them returned. Finally, he went and confronted Hujwiri himself, asking him to conjure up a miracle. Hujwiri replied, "I am not a juggler." Rai Raju began flying in the air, but Hujwiri ordered his shoes to bring him down. Rai Raju's shoes flew off and struck Rai Raju on his head, bringing him back to earth. Impressed and inspired by Hujwiri, he became his devotee, accepted Islam, and changed his name to Shaikh Ahmad Hindi. He is said to have succeeded Hujwiri after his death.

Hujwiri's last years were spent in Lahore, where he oversaw construction of a mosque and acquired many students and followers. He lived simply in a crowded lane of the Old City near the street of cobblers (*mochi gali*). After his death, his tomb became a refuge for wayfarers and other Sufis who came to Lahore to pay tribute to him: Dara Shikoh, Hazrat Mian Mir, Khwaja Muinuddin Chishti, Hazrat Nizamuddin Auliya, Baba Farid Ganj-i-Shakar, and Allama Iqbal, the poet philosopher of Pakistan, all swore allegiance to him.

The Data Ganj Bakhsh shrine complex that surrounds the tomb covers a large area with simple gardens, acres of marble, covered walkways where one can retreat when the sun is too hot, and many prayer places. At one end of the shrine is a newly constructed mosque with garish windows of dark glass and rocketlike minarets, a glaring contrast to the graceful Mughal-style architecture of the rest of the complex. In the sprawling courtyard thousands of people gather—praying, meditating, or simply waiting for the musicians who will perform the *qawwali* at sunset. Hundreds of people stand before the grave of Data Ganj Bakhsh, seeking the blessings of God and offering flowers and prayers. A large crowd encircles a man in a colorful turban who seems to be some sort of dervish. Throughout most of the day, there are lines of people accepting offerings of food from wealthier followers of the shaikh.

The Lord illuminated the hearts of the
pious with the light of certainty, which gave
them the vision to comprehend
the light of all faiths of the world.
  Hujwiri

To begin my visit I paid my respects to Data Sahib and asked for his blessings. Sitting in the courtyard and reflecting on my own discovery of the messages that different Sufis had brought to this land, I thought of the other spiritual seekers that came to Hujwiri's tomb in the course of their wandering. The grandson of the poet-philosopher Iqbal had told me that Iqbal had a vision for a separate Muslim homeland while meditating here at Hujwiri's tomb. Pilgrims from many different faiths spent days and weeks in meditation, reflecting on the *Kashf al-Mahjub* and the atmosphere of this ground where Data Ganj Bakhsh once preached. For many shaikhs and their disciples, a sojourn at this sacred place would inspire them and illuminate new paths to follow. Centuries after Data Sahib's time, his shrine is an eternal nexus in the spiritual landscape of this region. Mundane power can be so ephemeral, but true spiritual power will always emanate from the shrine of Data Sahib.

In his Persian poem "The Secrets of the Self," Iqbal sings:

With ease he broke the mountain-barriers
And sowed the seed of Islam in India.
The age of Omar was restored by his godliness,
The fame of the Truth was exalted by his words.
He was a guardian of the honour of the Koran,
The house of Falsehood fell in ruins at his gaze.
The dust of the Panjáb was brought to life by his breath,
Our dawn was made splendid by his sun.
He was a lover, and withal a courier of Love:
The secrets of Love shone forth from his brow.[8]

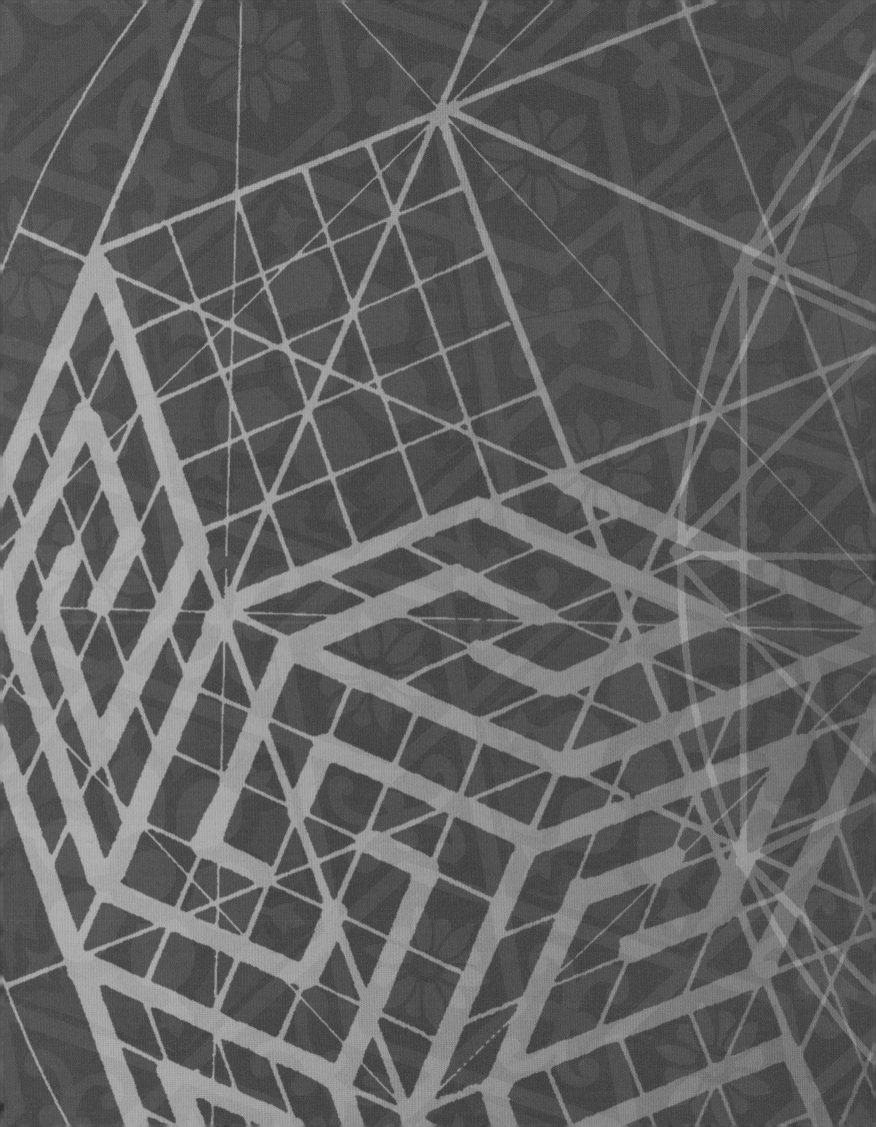

الا بذكر الله تطمئن القلوب

Verily in the remembrance of Allah do hearts find rest!

Qur'an 13:28

Be a blazing fire of Truth, be a beauteous blossom of love,
and be a soothing balm of peace.
With your spiritual light, dispel the darkness of ignorance;
Dissolve the clouds of discord and war and spread goodwill,
peace and harmony among the people.

Khwaja Muinuddin Chishti

Khwaja Muinuddin Hasan Chishti, Keeper of the Poor

My ancestral home was Ajmer, and my family often spoke of the importance of the shrine of Khwaja Muinuddin Hasan Chishti (CE 1141–1230; AH 53–627), a complex of buildings dedicated to the teachings of this *wali*, this saint, of Allah, whose major contribution was to spread the ethical and spiritual values of Islam. It was his humanism, disposition, and piety that won over the hearts of hundreds of thousands of people. He worked with the masses directly. He served and loved them, lived with them, and inspired them in the realization of Eternal Truth. Generations of my family owed allegiance to this shrine and continued Muinuddin's tradition of serving the poor. Having heard about these traditions all my life, I wanted to visit the shrine to learn about the shaikh and benefit from the *baraka*, the blessings and grace that everyone believed were still issuing forth from there:

> When the river pursues its course,
> the flow occasions force and noise,
> but when it ultimately merges into the sea,
> it rests in supreme peace.
>
> The same is true of the individual "self"
> covering various stages on its onward journey
> to merge itself in the Universal Self. [9]

I arrived in Ajmer on a hot and dusty afternoon and went directly to the shrine. My family had said that our custom was to pay respects to the shaikh before pursuing other obligations. The shrine is in the center of the town, surrounded by buildings that house pilgrims, a bazaar, and a mosque. Many of the monuments within the *dargah* complex were built by various rulers as a mark of their respect for the shaikh. I found I was one

149

of many people from all walks of life who had come to this place to seek blessings and plead for alleviation of their troubles. The enclave is accessed by walking through a bazaar filled with shops selling cloth *chadar*s stamped with religious sayings and embellished with calligraphy. As at other shrines, these *chadars* are often purchased by pilgrims to place on the graves in the complex along with offerings of flowers in commemoration of the teachings of the saint.

It is said that Islam was brought to India by Arab traders in CE 622 (AH 0), the same year the Prophet Muhammad and his followers left for Medina, and over time it became widely known and accepted through the ministry of traveling mystics who came from the holy lands of the Ottoman Empire. The growth of Islam and the task of inspiring the people to its tenets and values were accomplished in large part by Hazrat Khwaja Muinuddin Hasan Chishti, popularly known as Khwaja Sahib and Khwaja Gharib Nawaz ("Keeper of the Poor"). He apparently did not leave any written accounts, but the oral tradition about his teaching is strong. I obtained information about who he was from my family, from Ustaniji, and from the *sajjada-nashin*, the shaikh's current heir.

As at other shrines, there is a hierarchy of pious followers called *khadims* and *mutawalis* who regulate the various rituals at the shrine of Khwaja Sahib. I spoke to a *khadim* who described the daily ritual of cleaning the tomb. All the flowers and decorated cloth offerings are removed each day and are later distributed to the pilgrims as a blessing. The tomb is sprinkled with rose water and fresh flowers and cloths are again placed by the devout. I asked some visiting pilgrims why they had journeyed so far, and one of them replied: "Khwaja Muinuddin Chishti hears my entreaties. He was chosen by the Prophet to come and help us. He takes care of all of us unfortunates through his own great moral power, appealing character, love, and dedication to mankind, without any worldly resources of wealth, power, force, or support."

The *khadim* added, "To know the greatest mystic of all time, you should know a little bit about his life." He went on to recount that Khwaja Muinuddin Chishti was born in CE 1141 (AH 535) in Isfahan in southwestern Iran but later lived in Khorasan in the northeastern part of that country. According to the *khadim*, Muinuddin interpreted the true Islamic message of love for mankind, preached the Qur'anic philosophy of unity of religion, and worked out its potentialities for the whole of humanity. He laid the foundation of the liberal Chishti order of Sufis in India, inspired millions of souls to be his followers, and thus served the masses of the Indian subcontinent. He said to his followers,

Be a blazing fire of Truth, be a beauteous blossom of love, and be
a soothing balm of peace.
With your spiritual light, dispel the darkness of ignorance;
Dissolve the clouds of discord and war and spread goodwill,
peace and harmony among the people.[10]

According to legend, a revered monk named Shaikh Ibrahim Qunduzi
visited Muinuddin's orchard when he was a young man. Their exchanges
inspired Muinuddin to seek the heights of mystical experience. He
withdrew from the world, disposed of his property and other belongings,
and distributed his money to the poor. From Khorasan he traveled to
Samarkand in search of knowledge and higher education. He visited nearly
all the great centers of Muslim culture and acquainted himself with almost
every important trend in the Muslim religious life of his time.

It was common for Sufis to wander for years searching for a master with
whom they had an affinity that would allow complete surrender. The trials
that disciples encounter on the mystical path can only be navigated with the
help of a master who has become adept at the methods and exercises of the
Sufi doctrine. Muinuddin became the disciple of the Chishti saint Khwaja
Usman Harwani. They traveled the Middle East together and made visits to
Mecca and Medina. It was here, in the holy land of Arabia, that Muinuddin
dreamed that the Prophet Muhammad bade him travel to India. He stopped
at the shrine of Hujwiri to meditate, whereupon he experienced a vision
that directed him to go further into the desert and not stay in Lahore as
he had intended. Instead, he headed toward Rajasthan and stopped to rest
at Ajmer with his companions. Ajmer became the center from which the
Chishti order spread to other parts of India.

Kwaja Muinuddin Chishti used three principles as the basis of his
instruction: "a generosity like that of the ocean, a mildness like that of the
sun, and a modesty like that of the earth."[11] In his lifetime, he never turned
anyone away, and even today his shrine is accessible to all who would enter.
In Ajmer I witnessed a dynamic, living faith. Rituals and traditions of
Muslim life were being enacted within the shrine: a wedding, the blessing
of a newborn child, prayers for the departed. By the gate that led to the
courtyard of the tomb, where *qawwals* were chanting. I removed my shoes
and covered my head. Attendants to the shrine directed pilgrims around
the silver railings surrounding the tomb. It is believed that wishes made at
this tomb are granted, so people come from all over to make a wish. As at
Bhit Shah, the tradition is to tie a thread on the grilles of the marble screen,
and when the wish is granted to return offering money for the *langar* to feed
the poor. I was surprised to learn that many of the pilgrims here regarded

Khwaja as a living shaikh who is invisible but nevertheless present and able

to heal and give advice. This must be the reason that people keep coming here after hundreds of years while the monuments of kings are abandoned. The keepers of the shrine insist that the spirit of the shaikh can be felt if one is sincere in one's meditations.

I seated myself in the courtyard near the tomb and bowed my head. I was taught that my prayers should be addressed to Allah, so I was careful to articulate my desire for guidance directly to God, worried that offerings and wishes made at a shaikh's tomb might be *shirk*, a grave sin in Islam. I prayed for guidance, and as I slid into a state of meditation, I felt a presence behind me. I looked up to see an elderly man wearing a white cloth cap and white *kurta* (loose shirt) and pajamas standing there.

"I am one of the *khadims* here," he told me. "I assist with the maintenance and rituals at the shrine, and I have come here to help you accomplish your work."

"I came here to pray," I said, surprised. "Thank you anyway."

We talked about Khwaja Sahib and I learned more about his contributions to his *khanqahs*. Located in many large towns, *khanqahs* were spacious buildings where a group of Sufis could live together as a community of seekers. Visitors were always welcome, and many regarded themselves as "guests of God." There were smaller rooms in these places where individuals could retreat for long periods of meditation. It was believed that the company of likeminded people enhanced knowledge and helped one to keep on the path to Unity of Being, where one rejected materialistic concerns. Most *khanqahs* were endowed by the faithful, and the *langar-khana* at the *khanqah* in Ajmer was built by the Mughal emperor Akbar. A *langar-khana* is a kitchen in which atttendants cook food and distribute it to those who come to the shrine. This tradition continues to this day. Eating together like this is in marked contrast to the traditional caste system, which segregated people, another oft-cited reason for why Sufism attracts and welcomes followers of all faiths.

History tells us that emperors, rulers, and pilgrims both rich and poor have thronged to this oldest of Chishti shrines with their petitions, looking for solace. Because it is on the pilgrimage route to Delhi (home to the shrine of Shaikh Nizamuddin Auliya) and Pakpattan (the shrine of Baba Farid Shakar Ganj), many Sufis on their own quests come here to pray and meditate. Grateful pilgrims have erected buildings in and near the shrine as acts of faith, and it is today a lively place full of devotees from all faiths: Muslim, Hindu, Sikh, and Christian, who believe that *baraka*, or divine grace, and spiritual power linger around the tomb.

153

I listened to the *khadim* describe some of the ceremonies practiced here and found similarities to Mughal court culture: the offering of *nazr*, the gifts of food or valuables that are blessed and then distributed to the poor, the peacock feather fans used to dust the tombs. I later discovered that the patronage of noble Mughal devotees contributed funds and buildings. During the reign of the Mughal emperor Akbar (CE 1556–1605; AH 963–1013), Ajmer emerged as one of the most important centers of pilgrimage in India. It is said that in CE 1557 (AH 964), Akbar traveled from Agra to Ajmer to pay a visit to the *dargah* in fulfillment of a vow he had taken before launching his military campaign to subjugate the kingdom of Mewar. In Ajmer, Shah Jahan had proclaimed himself emperor after Jahangir's death as he was traveling from Udaipur to Delhi. Other Mughal emperors continued their homage, and to this day Ajmer witnesses the ebb and flow of history.

Accompanied by the *khadim*, I bought flowers from the flower seller and went to lay them as a mark of respect at the grave of Khwaja Sahib. I said the *fatiha* and prayed for peace. The *khadim* then asked me where we were staying, and I mentioned a hotel we had booked.

"Well, you must not stay there," he said. "You should stay at the rest house which overlooks the lake ... Do you know the legend of the lake? When Khwaja Sahib arrived in Ajmer with his few followers and wanted to camp under a bunch of shady trees outside the city wall near Anderkot, Raja Prithviraj's camel-keepers objected to his resting there. They insisted that the place was used as the stabling ground for the Raja's camels and that the strangers must move away to some other place. Actually, astrologers had warned the Raja that a dangerous dervish would enter his kingdom, and so the royal retainers were making certain that this band of travelers would be denied access. Khwaja Sahib, however, gracefully moved away to another site near the Anasagar Lake. But when the Raja's camels did not get up the next morning in spite of all efforts to make them move, the trouble was brought to the notice of Raja Prithviraj. He was much perturbed and is reported to have advised his men to approach Khwaja Sahib and seek a remedy by begging his pardon for having turned him out. When the camel-keepers did so, the Khwaja Sahib said: 'Go, the camels will get up.' On their return, they were surprised to find the camels standing."

We went with the *khadim* to the resthouse and were told that it was completely booked. The governor and his entourage were expected that afternoon. I was disappointed but I said my thanks and prepared to leave. The *khadim* said to me, "Bibi, do not go, you are meant to stay here. Let me get you some tea to refresh yourself." Then he disappeared.

157

I sat outside under a tree and looked at Anasagar Lake, appreciating the beautiful Mughal pavilions built long ago for visiting princes from Delhi. After an hour, the *khadim* appeared and said, "The governor has changed his plans, you may stay here." I was bemused by this unexpected turn of events and went to the suite reserved for the governor that looked out over the lake. I watched the sunset and thought about my family, who many generations ago had walked and prayed here. I also thought about being allowed to stay at the rest house. Was this a coincidence, or another wish granted by Khwaja Sahib? I was skeptical. But to the *khadim* who had befriended me, such supernatural incidents were commonplace. He told me of visions of angels rescuing people in distress, evil spirits that had been chased away by prayer, curses that had been neutralized. All this was a mixture of superstition and a belief in magic, and yet there was always the possibility that it was the result of the infinite power of God.

Perhaps rational explanations can take me only so far and no further. I saw again in my mind's eye the devotees at the shrine. Blind beggars, shrieking madmen talking to themselves, women tying threads and buying amulets, the boy who sat impassively behind the pile of shoes he was minding for pilgrims going into the shrine barefoot. The man who fell at my feet in a trance and then stood and twirled screaming, "Hu, Hu, Allah Hu." No one found this parade of humanity eccentric or wild. Truly, all were welcome.

I reflected on the harmony with which people of so many religious backgrounds met at the shrine to take part in the rituals. At the core of the tradition is the heart, the spirit of compassion. There was a deep sense of peace and oneness—singing together the mystical songs and eating together from the *dargah's langar-khana*. I wished that this acceptance of difference and ecumenical ethos could be exported into the wider world, a notion of justice, respect, and compassion against which we can measure our own behavior. I resolved to follow the mystical thread toward my own communion with God. It would be a long, difficult struggle to annihilate the ego. These visits to shrines seemed now to be preparation for the continuation of my journey beyond them.

UNTO ALLAH BELONG THE EAST AND THE WEST,

AND WHITHERSOEVER YE TURN,

THERE IS ALLAH'S COUNTENANCE.

QUR'AN 2:115

The fire of your separation has burnt our hearts.
The storm of desire to meet you has ravaged our lives.

Shaikh Fariddudin's greeting to Nizamuddin Auliya

Nizamuddin Auliya
and the Faqir Princess Jahanara

To the northeast of Ajmer lies Delhi, home to the tomb of one of the most beloved Sufis of the northern region of the subcontinent. Located in the Nizamuddin *basti* (settlement), the tomb of Nizamuddin Auliya (CE 1238–1325; AH 635–725) lies opposite to the Mughal emperor Humayun's tomb. The *basti* is a warren of lanes and houses squeezed together; one emerges at the end of the tunnel into the shrine's courtyard. Here, time stands still. The atmosphere is as it must have been for hundreds of years.

I was drawn to the environs of the shrine by the haunting strains of music that wafted over the densely crowded buildings. This was *qawwali*, the uniquely South Asian musical and vocal form of remembrance of God. The chants and repeated melodies induce in both the performer and the listener a better appreciation of divinity. In the courtyard itself, pilgrims were reading the Qur'an aloud or swaying to the rhythm of the recitation of the names of Allah, known as *zikr*. I sat among the people in the chamber that adjoins the tomb, where women were singing a *naat* (song) about Bibi Fatima, the daughter of the Prophet.

Hearing this song made me think of the role of women in Islam, which is rarely celebrated although their contributions to Islamic mysticism, in particular, are significant. For many Muslim women, the practice of pilgrimage is a central part of their piety. Through their poetry, their writings, and their work as teachers, women have played important roles throughout the ages. It was the women of my family who had set me on my own path of discovery. In their everyday lives they find consolation and spiritual uplift when they gather for worship or for making the food that they send to the *khanqah*. These daily acts of piety are part of our way of life.

I thought of the beginnings of Islam and of Bibi Khadija, the Prophet's first wife, an entrepreneur who supported his vision financially and spiritually when he was confronted with serious political and religious challenges. Their daughter, Fatima, is recognized as the first Muslim mystic because of her deep understanding of the mystical dimensions of Islam. She constantly sought a personal connection with the faith her father revealed to the Arab tribes.

Jalaluddin Rumi, Sufism's greatest mystical poet, often portrayed women as a symbol of the carnal self, *nafs*. This soul wanders along her tortuous path and endures many tribulations before being purified and united with the Beloved, who is God. This motif is central to the legends of the Indus Valley and the Punjab. In this folk literature, the protagonist is always a woman seeking her beloved and united with him in death, having survived many difficulties. These legends have been sung by bards, folksingers, and the common folk of the Indus Valley for eons. Each legend personifies human experience and mystical theories about unity with the Divine. The tragic tale of Sassi and Punnun had fired my imagination long before we had ever visited the shrine of Shah Abdul Latif. In Sufi thought, Sassi symbolizes selfless love, moral fortitude, and spiritual strength in the face of fatal adversity.

Women trained in the classical disciplines of Arabic history and mathematics appear throughout literature and history. One of the most prominent was Shah Jahan's daughter, the Mughal princess Jahanara. After the death of her mother, Mumtaz Mahal, Jahanara managed all the duties of state. Even while involved in affairs of state, however, she came to Nizamuddin's shrine to contemplate the divine mysteries. Mumtaz Mahal now lies in state in that most beautiful of architectural tributes to a great temporal love, the Taj Mahal, while her daughter rests in a simple tomb, buried out of spiritual love near the shrine of Nizamuddin, one of the Sufi shaikhs to whom her life was dedicated.

Jahanara journeyed from Lahore to Ajmer to Delhi pondering the messages of the mystics she encountered along the way. She was a devotee of the great Sufi teacher Muinuddin Chishti and a disciple of Sufi Mullah Shah Badakhshi. In both political and religious spheres, Jahanara refused to be a mere spectator from behind the veil. While occupied with the machinations of court life and the drama of royal succession, she managed to probe complex mystical problems in her writing. Through her patronage of Sufi ritual, scholarship, and architecture, she sought to chart a more active collaboration on the part of women in the development of religious thought and material culture.

In other forms of Islamic jurisprudence and religious interpretation, pre-Muslim local traditions of male superiority have eclipsed the Qur'anic affirmation of the importance of education for women. Jahanara's work, however, was well placed: indeed, Sufi tradition is one of the rare occurrences in which the original Qur'anic injunction of mutual respect and valuation of human beings regardless of gender has been preserved.

I have read Jahanara's poetry and studied her beautiful portrait in Mughal miniatures in many museums of the world. Here in Delhi I said a prayer for her soul as I stood before her small white marble tomb outside the shrine of Nizamuddin Auliya.

The paths of many Sufi shaikhs crossed in centers of spiritual learning before they established their own followings. I encountered them in unexpected places due to their widespread networks. Bakhtiar Kaki, the Sufi shaikh from Ferghana, had met Khwaja Muinuddin Chishti in Baghdad, where both were seeking spiritual instruction. Nizamuddin Auliya belonged to the same spiritual lineage as Muinuddin Chishti and Bakhtiar Kaki and represented the teachings of the Chishti order in Delhi. His Turkish grandfather had come to India from Bukhara and settled in the small town of Bada'un (in modern-day Uttar Pradesh), where Nizamuddin grew up. Nizamuddin studied in Delhi, both *hadith* (Prophetic tradition) and Arabic literature, and gained a reputation as a tenacious debater. A precocious student of the religious sciences, he was attracted early on by stories he heard from a wandering *faqir* about the great Sufi Fariduddin Ganj-i Shakar, the *khalifah*, or vice regent, of Bakhtiar Kaki, who had lived for a time in Delhi. Fariduddin's austerities and awe-inspiring demeanor were the stuff of legend. He often fasted for days at a time and secluded himself for periods of forty days to meditate. After one of these fasts, pebbles turned into sugar for him—hence his epithet Ganj-i Shakar, "Treasure of Sugar." Fariduddin's *khanqah* and spiritual center was located in Ajodhan on the Sutlej River, a place that was later known as Pakpattan, "the pure river crossing."

At the age of twenty, Nizamuddin traveled to Ajodhan in the Punjab to study the Qur'an, Sufism, and Islamic theology with Shaikh Fariduddin. To his astonishment, the master greeted him at their first meeting with a verse in which he declared that he had long awaited the coming of the young disciple:

The fire of your separation has burnt our hearts.
The storm of desire to meet you has ravaged our lives.[12]

Nizamuddin's instinct was that Shaikh Fariduddin was the perfect teacher for him, and he took initiation as the shaikh's disciple that very day.

Just three years later he was named successor to Fariduddin and returned to the Delhi suburb of Ghiyaspur, where he opened his doors to Muslims and Hindus alike. His teachings were about finding harmony and beauty by aspiring to spiritual fulfillment in the midst of the demands of everyday life. Dreams, relationships, desires, and ambitions can be realized with disciplined effort, he taught, by stepping away from egotism to a different spiritual dimension, allowing one to apprehend the higher reality of God.

> What power, what gain is there in turning a deaf ear to people and busying oneself with God? True benefit comes from remaining in the midst of people while constantly remembering God.[13]

Nizamuddin's eloquence and charismatic personality attracted many friends from all strata of society, and his influence led Sufism to became much more of a mass movement than it had been. His followers called him *Mahbub-i-Ilahi*, the Beloved of God. Among his good friends and disciples was the extraordinary Amir Khusrau (CE 1253–1325; AH 650–725), an administrator, philosopher, linguist, poet, scientist, and musician. As a student and chronicler of the languages of the Indus Valley, Khusrau felt the need for a language that would be accessible to the various nationalities at the Delhi court. He patronized and contributed to the development of a kind of subcontinental Esperanto, which he called "Hindvi." Over the course of history, two languages have developed from Khusrau's Hindvi: Urdu, the national language of Pakistan, and Hindi, the national language of India. Yet even this is not where Khusrau's most enduring fame lies.

Khusrau loved music passionately and was a singer of some renown. He also is popularly thought to be the inventor of the well-known stringed instrument, the *sitar*, and the Indian drum called the *tabla*. He became interested in the melodic structure of Hindu temple chants and the rhythms of the folk music of the Indus Valley, particularly of Sindh. Over the years, he evolved a style of music that involved an exploration of the material possibilities in a single theme (or *raga*) within the confines of a subtle rhythmic structure. This is, of course, the concept and basis of the best-known music of the subcontinent today—what is called, in the West, Indian classical music. The definition of its disciplines, modes, and forms was largely the work of Amir Khusrau, who also collected or composed the majority of the *ragas* on which this music is based.

Khusrau sought the tranquil and spiritual ambience of Nizamuddin's world as a refuge from the unsettled politics of Delhi at that time. As he spent more time in the company of Nizamuddin his poems acquired more spiritual dimensions. His poetry ranges from romantic epics to historical

177

tales, from military exploits of the rulers to mystical experiences under the tutelage of Nizamuddin.

Like his predecessors in the Chishti order, Nizamuddin wrote no books, though his teachings and sayings (*malfuzat*) were collected in diary form by the poet Amir Hasan Sijzi under the title *Morals for the Heart*. From this time onward, the genre of *malfuzat* became an important vehicle for spreading mystical ideas. The *malfuzat* also reflect the religious and social conditions of medieval India that are absent from official chronicles.

The following anecdote illustrates Nizamuddin's deep sympathy for the poor: Nizamuddin often turned away from the food he was offered, once remarking, "So many poor and destitute people are sleeping in the corners of the mosques and on the platforms of shops! They have nothing to eat for dinner. How can this food go down my throat?"[14]

Another story illustrates his extreme devotion to spiritual practice:

Every night [Nizamuddin] remained alone in his cell. He would bar the door and pass the hours in contemplation of the divine mysteries. When day broke, everyone who saw the glow on his face would think him to be intoxicated. … Amir Khusrau, who often saw him in this state, has captured the mood of the Shaykh's nocturnal piety in the following verse:

> You seem to be a reveler of the night—
> In whose embrace did you pass the night
> That even now your drunken eyes
> Show the effect of wine?[15]

Disturbed by Nizamuddin's popularity and his independence from rulers and the state, Sultan Alauddin Khilji (CE 1296–1316; AH 695–715), the second ruler of the Khilji dynasty of Delhi, became suspicious of the shaikh's political intentions. Alauddin chose his favorite son, Khizr Khan, to deliver a letter to Nizamuddin, since the prince was a disciple of the shaikh. Khizr Khan presented the document to him, but the shaikh left it unopened. He told his followers to recite the Sura al-Fatiha, and then

I cannot tell which abode it was,
The place where I spent the night;
All around the writhing of stricken lovers,
The place where I spent the night.

That beauty, her form,
Like a cypress tall, her face a tulip red;
Ah! What pain it gave to the heart,
The place where I spent the night.

My rivals attentive and she so proud,
And I stood trembling there;
It was hard to utter a word in the place
Where I spent the night.

God at the head of the gathered crowd;
And Khusrau lost in the Infinite;
Muhammad, the candle, that lit the throng,
In the place where I spent the night.
    Amir Khusrau

می دانم چه منزل بود شب جائیکه من بودم
بهر سو رقص سنبل بود شب جائیکه من بودم
پری پیکر نگارے، سرو قدے، لاله رخسارے
سراپا آفتِ دل بود، شب جائیکه من بودم
مرا از آتشِ عشق تو دامت سوخت اے خسرو
محمد شمع محفل بود شب جائے که من بودم
کلام امیر خسرو

replied: "We dervishes have nothing to do with the affairs of state, …
I have settled in a corner away from the men of the city and spend my time
in praying for the Sultan and other Muslims. If the Sultan does not like
this, let him tell me so. I will go and live elsewhere. God's earth is vast
enough."[16] When this news was related to the Sultan, he was overjoyed, and
in time he came to have great confidence in the shaikh.

When he knew he was dying, Nizamuddin requested that the poet
Amir Khusrau be buried with him. Nizamuddin passed away in CE 1325 (AH
725) at the age of 80, when Khusrau was away on a military campaign. On
his return to the city, Khusrau went to the grave site and said, "The fair one
lies on the couch with her black tresses scatterd [sic] on her face: O Khusrau,
come home now, for [night] has fallen all over the world."[17]

In *The Sufi Martyrs of Love*, Ernst and Lawrence cite the following
contemporary account of Nizamuddin's death:

For forty days before his death Shaykh Nizam ad-Din [Nizamuddin]
ate nothing. As the end approached, he said, "The time of prayer
has come; have I said my prayers?" If his followers replied, "Yes,
you have said them," then he would reply, "I must say them again."
He would perform every prayer twice, and add, "I am going, I am
going." He instructed his servant, Iqbal: "If anything of any sort
remains in this house, it will have to be accounted for on the Day
of Judgment. You must distribute everything, except the minimum
which is necessary for the daily subsistence of the dervishes." But
then he would correct himself: "These are the effects of a dead man,
why should they be preserved? Give it all away and sweep the room
clean." As soon as they cleared the storerooms, a host of people
gathered and snatched up the goods. Then the servants pleaded,
"But we are poor men. After you have gone, what will become of
us?" "The charity that will arrive at my grave will suffice for you,"
he rejoined. "Who will be able to divide it up among us?" they
asked. "That man who is able to relinquish his own portion," was
the shaykh's reply.[18]

179

At his burial, Nizamuddin's disciples covered his body with the cloak that he had received from Shaikh Fariduddin and put his prayer mat under his head. Nizamuddin wished to be buried in the open but Sultan Muhammad ibn Tughluq built a dome over the grave and his son, Firuz Shah ibn Tughluq, built an enclosure with doors and screens. Many other rich and titled devotees continued the work of embellishing the tomb and today it is a vast complex with a mosque, *madrasah*, dwellings for the *khadims*, and other mausoleums.

While I was immersed in thoughts of Nizamuddin the *qawwali's* lyrics captured my attention. I closed my eyes and let the praise of Allah wash over me. I must seek the path of purifying the heart, I thought, as the words of Amir Khusrau remind us:

I cannot tell which abode it was,
The place where I spent the night;
All around the writhing of stricken lovers,
The place where I spent the night …

God at the head of the gathering crowd
And Khusrau lost in the Infinite
Muhammad, the candle, that lit the throng
In the place where I spent the night.[19]

I DO NOT RESIDE ON THE EARTH NOR IN THE HEAVENS
BUT I RESIDE IN THE HEART OF THE TRUE BELIEVER.

HADITH

لايسعني في الأرض ولا في السماء
ولكن يسعني في قلب عبدي المؤمن

God looks not at your forms, nor at your deeds,
but He looks at your hearts.

    Rukn-i-Alam

Shaikh Rukn-i-Alam, the Pillar of the World

Multan has been for three centuries an important outpost of Sufi Islam. Located between Sindh and Punjab, it lies on a major pilgrimage route that winds south from Lahore to Sindh. It is known as "The City of Sufis" because the magnificent shrines and mausoleums of the Sufis dominate the skyline of this bustling industrial city, their glittering blue tiles shimmering in the heat.

Shaikh Rukn-i-Alam (CE 1251–1335; AH 648–735) is buried in Multan in one of the most impressive tombs in the subcontinent, a building that attempts to match in physical presence the spiritual power of the saint. Its huge white dome sits near the main gate of Multan fort and can be seen from miles around. Built on an octagonal plan, its blue and white tiles stand out against the red brick façade. The mausoleum is the site of pilgrimage for over 100,000 pilgrims annually from all over South Asia who come to commemorate the memory of Rukn-i-Alam.

The old walls of the city are still here, but they are unable to contain the sprawling settlement. New buildings insensitive to the design of the Tughluqs and Mughals exist side by side with the older monuments. Even so, each mausoleum remains a resting place for wandering pilgrims and for the local population, and each serves as a reminder of the teachings of the sages. These sanctuaries are also the places where the yearly *urs* are held, the occasions when most pilgrims converge on the city. Otherwise the rhythm of daily life continues. Scholars and poets, musicians and ordinary people pass through as they always have. My visit to this imposing series of tombs began with conversations with the custodians who put into perspective the history that shapes the experience of a contemporary pilgrim.

189

In the twelfth and thirteenth centuries CE (sixth and seventh centuries AH), Sufism began to take shape as an institution through the establishment of new *silsilas,* the lineage chains of charismatic shaikhs who were the leading teachers of the time. These individuals traveled throughout the Muslim lands seeking knowledge of God. Along their routes of travel, lodging houses sprang up and became places where seekers could gather to share their experiences. Gradually these evolved into the *khanqahs* that are affiliated with the various orders.

The great pioneers of this Sufi movement were the four friends and contemporaries: Shaikh Fariduddin Masud Ganj-i-Shakar of Pakpattan (CE 1174–1266; AH 569–664), Shaikh Syed Jalaluddin Bukhari of Uch-Bahawalpur (CE 1196–1294; AH 592–693), Shaikh Bahauddin Zakariya of Multan (ca. CE 1182–1262; AH 578–660), and Shaikh Lal Shahbaz Qalandar of Sehwan (CE 1177–1274; AH 572–672).

The Suhrawardi order was the first to arrive in the Indus region. It was founded in Baghdad by Shaikh Shihabuddin Suhrawardi and brought to Multan by Bahauddin Zakariya. Shaikh Fariduddin and Shaikh Bahauddin were friends who lived a few miles from each other. Fariduddin was an ascetic and spurned royal patronage, while Bahauddin was a prosperous landlord who kept company with the ruling classes. The poet Fakhruddin Iraqi lived with Bahauddin's entourage for some twenty-five years, writing love lyrics. Annemarie Schimmel tells us that "the tender and intoxicating love poems that the Persian poet composed are still being sung by Pakistani musicians" at the door of Bahauddin's tomb in Multan.[20]

Gradually, but particularly during the time of the Mughals, Sufism in this region became entwined with local social and political life. In return for providing spiritual guidance and moral authority, certain Sufis of the Suhrawardi order gained considerable political power. One of these outstanding personalities was Shaikh Ruknuddin Abu al-Fath, popularly known as Rukn-i-Alam, the "Pillar of the World." Unlike the Chishti *silsilas,* which elected their successors, the Suhrawardi Sufis passed succession from father to son, and Rukn-i-Alam was the disciple and successor of his father, Shaikh Sadruddin Arif, and his grandfather, Shaikh Bahauddin Zakariya.

Rukn-i-Alam inherited his father's mantle in his mid-thirties, and continued his scholarship and spiritual leadership while playing a highly visible role in public affairs. His relations with the reigning sultans were excellent. Alauddin Khilji of Delhi twice gave him thousands of coins, which the shaikh immediately distributed to the poor. It seems that Rukn-i-Alam suffered from an infirmity that required him to be carried on a sedan chair, and when he went to visit Sultan Qutbuddin Mubarak, the people of Delhi would attach their petitions to his chair. In this way, he conveyed to the sultan the requests of the poor and the destitute so that their needs could be met. There is a Sufi tradition that says the shaikh would not leave the sultan's court until all the petitions were granted.[21]

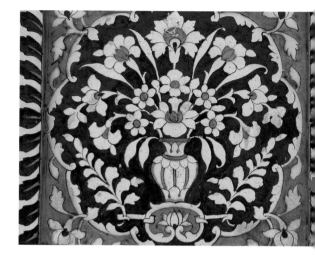

Rukn-i-Alam had close relations with other Sufis of his day, especially the Chishti master Nizamuddin Auliya. It is said that the Sultan was not on good terms with Nizamuddin, and he invited Rukn-i-Alam to his court in order to favor him and snub Nizamuddin. Hearing of the invitation Nizamuddin came a good distance out of the city to welcome Rukn-i-Alam. When Rukn-i-Alam went to court, the Sultan asked him if anyone from the city had come to meet him. He said, "The best person in the city," meaning the respected Sufi master Nizamuddin.

On another occasion an interesting exchange of learning and courtesy took place at a meeting between the two shaikhs in the great mosque of Delhi. One of Rukn-i-Alam's disciples asked the reason for the Prophet's emigration from Mecca to Medina. Rukn-i-Alam replied that the reason was that some of the perfections and ranks of prophecy had been suspended from operation in the world of action until the Prophet could go to meet the Medina ascetics known as the People of the Bench (*ahl al-suffa*). Nizamuddin said that the reason was the *faqirs* of Medina, who so far had been deprived of meeting the Prophet, and who would now have that benefit.

Sufis say that through these answers the two shaikhs were showing their humility and respect toward each other. Rukn-i-Alam professed that he had come to Delhi to perfect himself and benefit from being in the company of Nizamuddin, who in turn replied that Rukn-i-Alam came for the benefit of Nizamuddin. The two continued to have many cordial encounters, and Rukn-i-Alam presided over Nizamuddin's funeral.

I wondered about other discussions Nizamuddin might have had with Rukn-i-Alam, imagining the two shaikhs conversing as they reclined on white sheets, with candles burning and pigeons rustling their wings outside.

Unfortunately, in the case of Rukn-i-Alam, it has been difficult to get an idea of his teachings because of the unavailability of any writings by him or his followers. Carl W. Ernst told me that Abdulhaqq Dihlawi had access to two collections of the sayings of Rukn-i-Alam made by his followers: *al-Fatawa al-Sufiya* ("Decrees of the Sufis") and *Majma al-Akhbar* ("Collected News"). He explained that these writings are now supposed to have been lost, although it seems that the former exists in Arabic but has hardly been studied.[22]

Carl recounted the following description of ethical purification recorded by Abdulhaqq in *Majma al-Akhbar*:[23]

Recalling a familiar Sufi adage, Rukn-i-Alam divides humanity into three types: seekers of this world who follow their desires, seekers of the afterlife who long for paradise, and seekers of God who want nothing else besides God. Ethical purification is the replacement of worldly desires by the higher virtues. Rukn-i-Alam describes the human being as having two aspects, the inner nature and the outer form. The inner nature is not visible to the human eye, and likewise, "God looks not at your forms, nor at your deeds, but He looks at your hearts." The true nature of one's soul only becomes evident with the heightened state of consciousness associated with the resurrection. Everyone will be resurrected in the form corresponding to his nature. In this way, the tyrant and oppressor sees himself in the form of the wolf, the arrogant man in the form of the leopard, and the greedy miser in the form of the pig.

Rukn-i-Alam went on to say that as long as men are not purified from these defects, they will be worse than beasts.

Purification of the soul can only be achieved by divine mercy, the first sign of which is that one can finally see the faults in one's soul. "Then within him glows a spark of the lights of divine majesty, next to which all existing things vanish away, so that the world and all its greatness becomes dust in his eyes." When this condition occurs, one necessarily turns away from the animalistic qualities in which the masters of the world are imprisoned, and tries to replace those qualities with angelic ones.

I understood from this teaching that if one succeeds in purifying the soul, the qualities of forgiveness, mildness, humility, generosity, and liberality will appear in place of injustice, anger, pride, avarice, and greed. This ethical purification is, however, still only the practice of the seekers of the afterlife; the work of the seekers of God is something higher than this. They follow the saying of the Prophet, "Adopt the qualities of God," though not everyone understands this level of attainment. I knew that for me this was a humble beginning.

من صفاء الحب

فلوصاون جنتيا صفاء

فلو صاون حبيبا

فلو صوفي (قل)

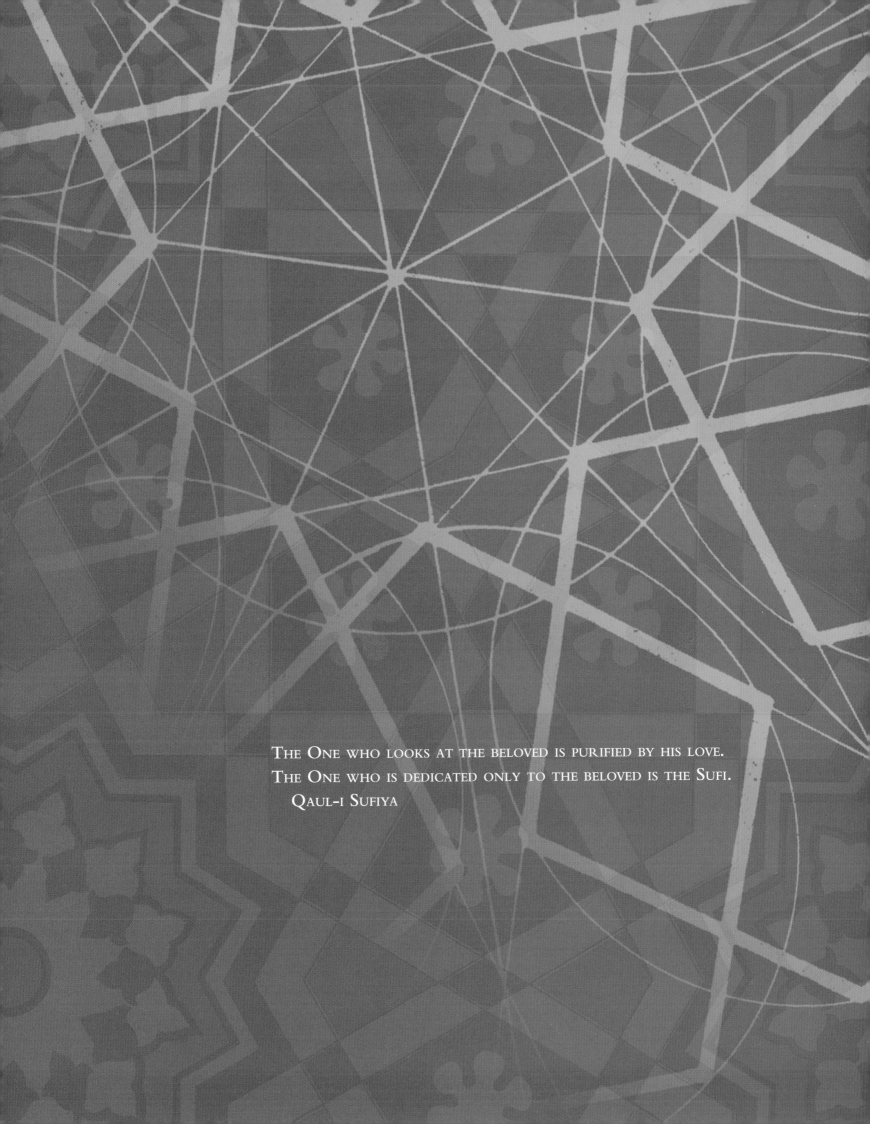

THE ONE WHO LOOKS AT THE BELOVED IS PURIFIED BY HIS LOVE.
THE ONE WHO IS DEDICATED ONLY TO THE BELOVED IS THE SUFI.
QAUL-I SUFIYA

Without the beloved, nights have become vast,
shedding flesh, shed to a skeleton,
bones crackle, I am demassed;
Without the beloved, nights have become vast.

   Madho Lal Husain

Madho Lal Husain

and the Festival of Lamps

When I revisited Lahore in the course of my pilgrimage, I discovered many shrines as I wandered around the city, and I began to learn the history of the folk poets and Sufi seekers who have made Lahore and its environs their home. I was invited to a musical evening dedicated to the music of Shah Husain at the home of Syed Najam, a remarkable man who has spent his life studying the *kafi* (layered verses) and the music of Punjab's gifted poets. Syed Najam's living room floor is covered with white sheets, and pillows and bolsters are set against the walls. The simplicity of the room is a perfect setting for musicians whose passionate voices stir the listeners. Everyone sits respectfully, and many close their eyes as the music washes over them.

Even if one does not understand the Punjabi words, the intention and the inspiration in the lyrics come through. The *kafi* I heard that evening revolved around the central theme of developing self-knowledge before even approaching the journey toward knowing God. The language and the lyrics lend themselves to numerous interpretations from the literal to the allegorical. Shah Husain used poetry to express his ecstatic longing. It was after the performance that we discussed the story of this poet.

The scholars there that evening told me the history of Husain, who was born in CE 1538 (AH 944) in Lahore into an extremely poor family of what was possibly the Dhudha Rajput tribe. The Sufis had converted many members of such tribes in the southern Punjab from the fifteenth century CE onward. Husain's father was a weaver by trade but he himself was not taught the craft. Instead, he was encouraged to study. At the age of ten, he memorized the entire Qur'an and became a *hafiz*. Initiated into the Qadiri Sufi order, Husain went to the shrine of Ali Hujwiri, popularly known as Data Ganj Bakhsh, to study Sufism. He remained there for twelve years.

When he was twenty-six, Husain became a student of Shaikh Sadullah and continued his studies in Sufism. It is said that during his studies with Sadullah, Husain came across the Qur'anic verse (29:64), "The life of this world is nothing but a game and a sport." The shaikh explained that this meant that the world we know is transitory, a mere game of the cosmos. Husain, however, thought the words of the verse were about freeing man from the rigid rules imposed by the *ulema*, the religious authorities. He told his teacher that, in accordance with his own interpretation of the verse, he would spend the rest of his life seeking God's understanding rather than fearing his wrath.

It is also said that Husain expressed his devotion through singing, dancing, and wearing *lal*, red clothes, and thus became known as Lal Husain. He was a popular mystic and teacher, known and recognized even by Emperor Akbar, during whose reign Husain became consumed with the love of the Divine.

During his time as a preacher, Husain encountered a young Brahmin boy named Madho Lal, who showed interest in his teachings. Husain recognized the radiance of divine beauty in this boy, and folk legends tell of the close relationship that developed between them—a relationship that became the subject of much speculation and controversy. In Punjabi, *lal* also means "ruby" and is the symbol of something precious. Husain addressed a *kafi* to Madho in which he referred to the boy as Lal. Their relationship was so profound that their names have been joined, and they are sometimes thought of as one person, Madho Lal Husain.

Husain's love and friendship for people of all castes and faiths were reflected in his deeply tolerant attitude toward others. It is said that once while watching the celebration of the Hindu festival of Holi, Madho, who was Hindu, threw colored powder at Husain, who proceeded to join in the fun. Husain took to celebrating this festival enthusiastically every year. He is said to have asserted that he was neither a Muslim nor a pagan, and he had close spiritual links with the Hindu mystic Chaju Bhagat and with Guru Arjun of the Sikhs.

Husain is widely known as the first mystical poet to compose ecstatic songs in his native Punjabi. His profound love for the Divine had a significant impact on his vivid poetry, which talks not only of love, but also of longing. Calling on popular folk tradition to express his feelings, he used the image of a woman craving for union with the Divine Beloved:

Without the beloved, nights have become vast,

shedding flesh, shed to a skeleton,

Madho Lal Husain.
Unknown artist and date.

مادهولال حسین

bones crackle, I am demassed;
Without the beloved, nights have become vast.[24]

Husain died in CE 1599 (AH 1007) in Shahdara and was buried there. However, several years later the Ravi River flooded and his grave was swept away. It is said that Madho brought the corpse to Baghbanpura in Lahore, where it was buried once again. After his death, Madho was buried at Husain's side.

Tucked away in a small square at the end of a series of winding lanes dotted with stalls, the shrine of Madho Lal Husain is near Lahore's Shalimar Gardens. Every year in March, thousands of devotees gather here to commemorate Husain's *urs*, during which the Mela Charaghan, or Festival of Lamps, is held for three days. The *mela* is a vibrant folk festival with all sorts of distractions: musicians, soothsayers, mendicants, *faqirs*, and performers. The neighborhood outside the shrine fills with pilgrims, and Husain's *kafis* are sung continuously for the three days of the festival. On the last day, women gather to pay their respects, and sing and dance to express their devotion. People lay floral wreaths and *chadars* and throw rose petals over the two raised tombs. Incense, smoke, and clouds of hashish mingle as the crowds gather around the fire pit—whose flames symbolize the immolation of the ego—and dance to the incessant and deafening beat of the drums.

Everywhere, people disembark from rickshaws and buses and trucks. Many travel from villages and towns far removed from Lahore. Devotees light lamps and candles at Husain's shrine, and supplicants believe that throwing candles into the fire pit will assure that their wishes will be granted. Rows of pilgrims move forward slowly, saying prayers, placing their offerings at the graves, then moving on again. The sanctuary is lit with blazing lights. Mounds of rose petals add their heady perfume to the incense that is burning in the holders at every corner. People pause at the flower-smothered tombs, each one saying a prayer, lighting a candle, or placing cloth stamped with calligraphic prayers in the sanctuary.

Outside in the courtyard, the sounds of the flute, the *tabla*, and the harmonium weave intricate harmonies. The lead singer's voice rises, commanding the pilgrims' attention. He throws back his head and sings the invocation; then the musicians who accompany him join their voices in chorus into the rhythmic structures of the *qawwali*. Several pilgrims dance the *dhamal*. The drums beat in wild abandon and from many throats comes the cry: "Shah Husain, *wali* of Allah, Shah Husain!"

As I leave the shrine with its throngs of devotees, its hustle and noise, I remember that Shah Husain came from a family of weavers, as did Kabir,

another renowned mystic and a weaver who lived in this region some forty years before Husain. The rigid caste system of the time placed weavers below the low-caste peasants who worked the land. Shah Husain resisted and defied the hierarchies of caste and the divisions of faith, and so I find it fitting that his death anniversary is celebrated with a local folk festival with Hindu and Sikh origins, and that the imagery of weaving is so prevalent in his writings. The pilgrims who come to honor him wear a great variety of fabrics of every imaginable color. The interdependence of peoples, traditions, and faiths, I think, is a metaphorical tapestry woven with many colors and hues, the warp and the weft incorporating all of society. The experience of the sacred is intricately woven throughout the world that surrounds us.

الَا إِنَّ أَوْلِيَاءَ اللَّهِ لَا خَوْفٌ عَلَيْهِمْ وَلَا هُمْ يَحْزَنُونَ

Lo! Verily the friends of Allah are those on whom fear cometh not, nor do they grieve.
Qur'an 10:62

For those who have love's pain,
the only cure is seeing the Beloved.

Mian Mir

It is dawn in Lahore and the sleeping city slowly comes to life. A fine mist floats over the garden of the house where I am staying. The cool breeze brings with it echoes of the past of this city of gardens and saints. As I set off toward the old British cantonment area, the call to prayer resonates among the rooftops of the town.

I walk through winding streets from Allama Iqbal Road to the shrine of Mian Mir. The small brick houses crowd together before the road opens to the gate of the *khanqah* adjacent to the shrine. Archways of pale pink stone frame the north and south entrances to the courtyard. As I pass through the gate, pigeons fly out of their roosts and settle on the small dome that crowns the final resting place of this revered saint.

On the western side of the courtyard I see a mosque. The graves of the saint's close relatives and disciples are located across the courtyard to the east, and a larger graveyard extends to the south and west. The majestic canopy of a great leafy tree dominates the courtyard. I walk up the white stone pathway toward the square green structure of Mian Mir's elevated mausoleum, its white dome embellished with fine Mughal frescos and ceramic tiles. The tomb's surface seems to come to life as I approach to pay my respects.

Mir Muhammad, known as Mian Mir, came to Lahore when he was twenty-eight and remained here for the rest of his life. Born in CE 1550 (AH 957) in Sehwan in Sindh, where his maternal grandfather lived, Mian Mir felt an impulse toward spirituality early in his life. His mother, Bibi Fatima, was a daughter of the famous Sindhi saint Qadi Qadan, a great mystical poet of this region, and was an important Sufi in her own right. She instructed Mian Mir in the teachings of the Qadiri order, which—through the efforts of Mian Mir, his sister Jamal Khatun, and his disciples—experienced a renaissance that spread throughout northern Punjab and eventually became an extensive Sufi community. The influence of women mystics resonates as deeply as that of their male counterparts in this branch of Sufism.

Few religious figures in the Indian subcontinent have had the influence that Mian Mir did, not only on the highest levels of society, but also across religious lines. A recluse throughout his life, Mian Mir exerted himself to the utmost to achieve detachment from worldly desires, and it was this inner independence that won him the respect of all classes and faiths. Among the Mughal emperors, Jahangir was the first to become interested in his teachings. "Mian Mir carefully observed the injunctions of the Qur'an and the example of the Prophet," Annemarie Schimmel tells us. "His spiritual power impressed Jahangir and Shah Jahan, and Prince Dara Shikoh was brought into his presence when he was seriously ailing and was healed."[25]

Dara Shikoh, the son and heir of Shah Jahan, became deeply attached to Mian Mir. He and his older sister, Princess Jahanara, were officially initiated into the Qadiri order in CE 1639 (AH 1048) by Mullah Shah Badakhshi, who became the *khalifah*, successor to the spiritual leadership, after Mian Mir's death in CE 1635 (AH 1044). Mullah Shah thought so highly of Jahanara's spiritual development that he considered her worthy of being his *khalifah*—but the Qadiri order forbade female successors. In CE 1642 (AH 1051), Dara Shikoh wrote a collection of biographical accounts of Qadiri saints, *Sakinat al-Awliya* ("The Peace of the Saints"), from which one can get a fairly vivid picture of the saint and the environment in which he lived. Dara was also very close to Bibi Jamal Khatun, Mian Mir's sister, who was admired for her piety and asceticism, and he gave her biography special prominence by placing it immediately after that of Mian Mir in his writings.

After Mian Mir's death, Dara Shikoh began to gather materials to build a tomb for the saint, but failed to complete it. He was defeated in a bitter war of succession with his brother Aurangzeb and was executed for apostasy in CE 1659 (AH 1069). In the end, however, Aurangzeb's regard for Mian Mir outweighed his hatred for his brother, and he ordered the completion of the imposing tomb that so many visit today. Dara once wrote, "In the prime of my youth a voice from the Unseen addressed me four times saying: 'God will give you something that has not been conferred on any emperor of the world.'"[26] Indeed, his legacy has endured far longer than that of most emperors and kings. His literary contributions continue to inspire intellectuals worldwide. Among them is his great translation of the Upanishads into Persian, a work that Annemarie Schimmel credits with influencing European philosophers and thinkers. "Throughout the nineteenth century," she wrote, "the Upanishads remained one of the most sacred textbooks for many German and German-influenced thinkers. Its mystical outlook has, to a large extent, helped to form in the West the image of India ..."[27]

Mian Mir, too, was a man of considerable learning, consulted by scholars throughout his life. He was steeped in Ibn Arabi's mystical philosophy of *wahdat al-wujud,* the Unity of Existence. His wisdom was disseminated by his disciples through the oral tradition of *malfuzat,* the sayings and discourses they repeated and sometimes recorded. Mian Mir's personal qualities and values were demonstrated by his simple lifestyle, which consisted of praying, teaching, meditating, and the practice of *zikr*—the constant repetition of the profession of faith. *Zikr* is a physical act of remembering God through repeated invocations and has been made popular through the rituals of the Qadiri order. By repeatedly invoking God, the disciple gradually strips himself of ego so that he can be closer to God.

At Mian Mir's shrine I sat with the circle of pilgrims and recited prayers with them for several hours. Once my mind stilled in contemplation, the *zikr* became a communication with the Divine, an awareness of the Absolute, and an attempt to lead will and intelligence back to God. I felt with humility that the love spoken of here was an all-consuming, self-annihilating love, a denial of the self. The enormity of the realization engulfed me and I recognized, once again, how long the road before me was, and how inadequate my preparation.

Mian Mir had no interest in the trappings of saintly authority; he called his disciples "friends" rather than followers, and he pursued his spiritual goal with single-minded concentration. He frequently quoted with approval the saying of the Prophet, "There is no real prayer except with the presence of the heart." I understand this to mean that one's innermost being should reflect the attributes of the Divine. For most Sufis, the paradigm of the perfect soul and being is the Prophet Muhammad and we should strive to mirror his example. As the Qur'an (4:80) states, "Whoever obeys [Muhammad] obeys God."

Within Mian Mir's philosophy can be found the first condition of the path of love: Give up this world and the next, and let them go. As Ibn Arabi said, "the Lord of the Heavens ... send[s] [mysteries] to the heart of anyone [with] purity ... Remove from your thought the exterior of words, seek the interior ... until you understand." He also wrote, "He knows

227

I was enamoured of studying books on the ways of the men of the Path and had in my mind nothing save the understanding of the Unity of God; and before this, in a state of ecstasy and enthusiasm, I had uttered some words pertaining to sublime knowledge, because of which certain bigoted and narrow-minded people accused me of heresy and apostasy. It was then that I realised the importance of compiling the aphorisms of great believers in the Unity of God and the sayings of saints who have, hitherto, acquired knowledge of Reality, so that these may serve as an argument against those who are really imposters.

Dara Shikoh
Hasanat ul-'Arifin ("The Aphorisms of the Gnostics")

Portrait of Dara Shikoh.
Mughal, c. seventeenth century CE.

دارا شكوه

Himself by Himself ... other-than-He cannot grasp Him."[28] The custodians of Mian Mir's shrine told me that when he was lying on his deathbed, a noble of the Mughal court, Wazir Khan, came to him and wanted to give him some medicine. Mian Mir is said to have replied, "For those who have love's pain, the only cure is seeing the Beloved." Both Mian Mir and Ibn Arabi knew that there is no Being other than the Being of God; there is no Reality other than the Reality of God. Each individual must renounce the ego and submit to the will of Allah.

Mian Mir disdained the commercial side of official Sufi shrines, with their large incomes derived from donations. But his followers, common folk and kings alike, have celebrated and enshrined his memory by building and tending the tomb that bears his name. I wondered at this irony as I sat in the courtyard and imagined Mian Mir sitting under the massive tree instructing his royal disciples. I remembered a collection of miniature paintings in the Lahore Museum that show Mian Mir—white-bearded, dignified, and austere—standing with Shah Jahan, Dara Shikoh, and Mullah Shah. But Mian Mir's "friends" came from all walks of life.

Mian Mir was so universally respected that Arjun, the fifth Guru of the Sikhs, asked him to lay the foundation stone for the holiest site of the Sikhs, the Golden Temple in Amritsar. The current custodians of Mian Mir's tomb point to this fact with particular pride. The Sikh scriptures also record Mian Mir's unsuccessful attempt to save Guru Arjun's life after the Sikh leader incurred the wrath of Emperor Jahangir by sheltering the rebel prince Sultan Khusrau in CE 1605 (AH 1013). Subsequently, during the period of Sikh rule in the Punjab, Ranjit Singh typified Sikh attitudes by preserving the tomb of Mian Mir at a time when other Muslim monuments suffered damage.

The Qur'an (2:256) says "there can be no compulsion in religion," and Islam is, for me, a religion of diversity. Aspects of Sufi doctrine may

230

be formulated quite differently from one Sufi to another, but Mian Mir,
Mullah Shah, and Dara Shikoh all found ways to view the same reality.
I paused to contemplate my own journey and the gifts I had received
that could not be measured by material means. The sun was warm. Light
filtering through the leaves made patterns on the stone terrace. Feeling
refreshed in spirit, I passed under the archway back into the "worldly"
neighborhood, carrying with me an infusion of gratitude and a resolve to
remember the pluralism and religious tolerance that Mian Mir professed.

With a prayer for Mian Mir's teaching to touch all hearts, I recalled the
words of the poet-philosopher, Iqbal:

The flute of Love's music—
His tomb protects our city from all harm.

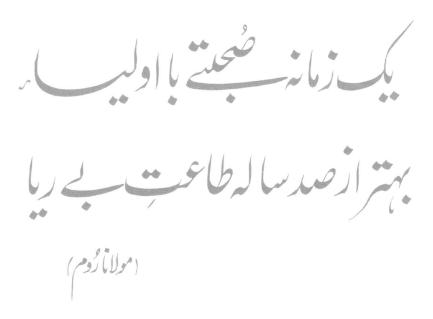

یک زمانہ صحبتے با اولیا
بہتر از صد سالہ طاعتِ بے ریا
(مولانا رُوم)

One moment of interaction with saints
is better than one hundred years of worship in hypocrisy.

Rumi

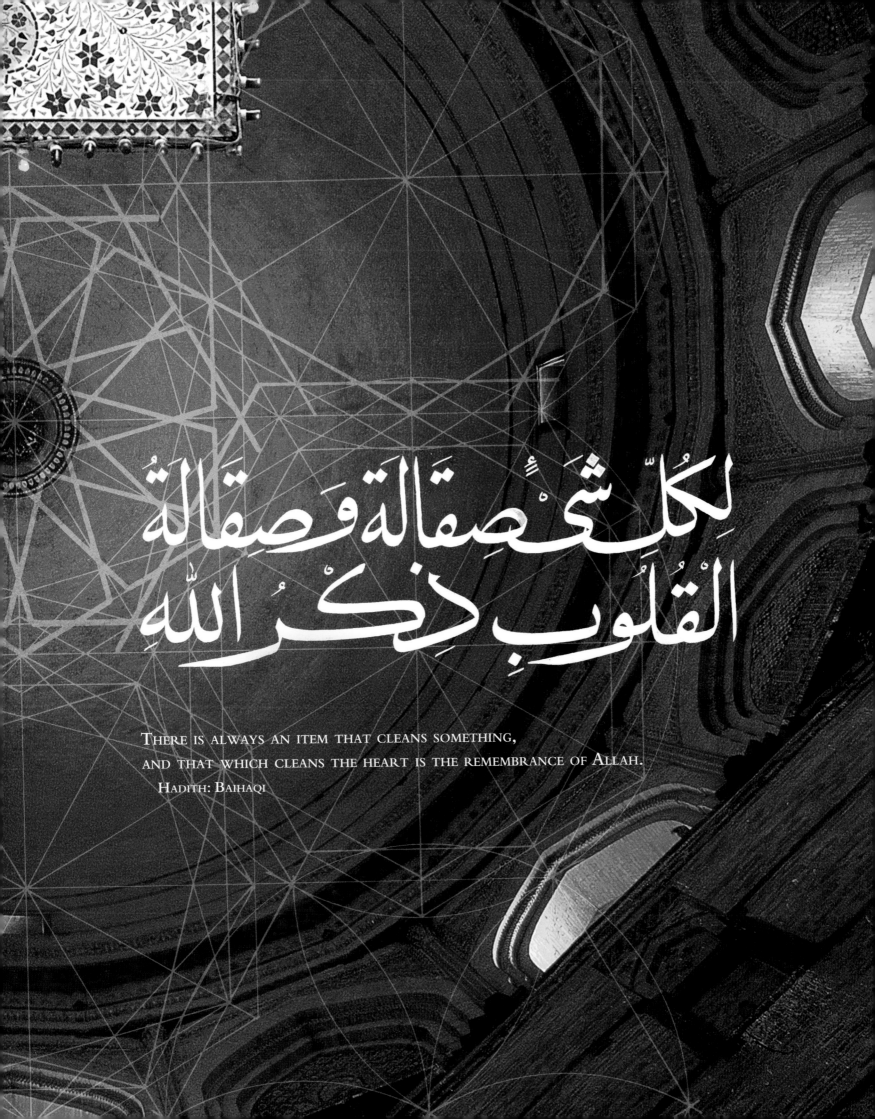

لِكُلِّ شَيءٍ صِقَالَةٌ وَصِقَالَةُ الْقُلُوبِ ذِكْرُ اللَّهِ

THERE IS ALWAYS AN ITEM THAT CLEANS SOMETHING,
AND THAT WHICH CLEANS THE HEART IS THE REMEMBRANCE OF ALLAH.
HADITH: BAIHAQI

I have got lost in the city of love,
I am being cleansed, withdrawing myself
from my head, hands and feet.
I have got rid of my ego, and have attained my goal.
Thus it has all ended well.

    Bulleh Shah

The Mystical Poetry
of Bulleh Shah

The landscape changes as I travel west along the Ravi, and the monuments in the small towns and villages remind me that here, people and ideas and religions have met and mingled for centuries. Everywhere there are vestiges of *pirs*, *faqirs*, and dervishes. Popular songs play on the car radio, and every village has music blaring in the market square. These songs and the new "rock" versions of the *kafis* of Bulleh Shah are familiar to me, the beloved lyrics performed by young bands of musicians.

One hour from Lahore is the village of Kasur. At the center of the town, just off the main street, is the shrine of Bulleh Shah. He was a much-loved folk poet whose soulful verses are still sung by many—including the gifted and popular Pakistani singer Abida Parveen, who draws inspiration from Bulleh Shah's poetry. These *kafis* and poems are examples of what mystics endeavor to do: simply to teach the love of God and the Prophet without becoming enmeshed in theological debate. Such verses, written in the local languages, were a bridge to the masses who were not learned in Arabic and Persian, the languages of the elite.

The layered verses of mystical poetry operate at several levels. Recognizable folk legends, imagery, and metaphor represent the Sufi quest for unity with the Divine. Some *kafis* remove gender as a divider of mankind. Through the poetry, illiterate villagers were led to an understanding of basic Islamic values, among them trust and unquestioning faith in God's wisdom:

> Every moment love's new surge of spring
> When the ways of love-rapture I gained
> Differences of me and you were not sustained
> The shell and pith were washed clean, unstained

Wherever I look the friend is befriending
Every moment love's a new surge of spring.[29]

A defiant rebel, Bulleh Shah is a controversial figure even today. I
learned much about him from Muzaffar Ghafaar, a poet in Lahore who
has studied the history and culture of the Punjab and is compiling a
comprehensive collection of the masterworks of Punjabi Sufi poetry.

Bulleh Shah was born Abdullah Shah in CE 1680 (AH 1090) (d. CE
1758; AH 1171). His father, Shah Muhammad Dervish, spoke Arabic and
Persian and studied and taught the Qur'an. Bulleh Shah began his education
learning from his father at the village mosque in Pandoke. As a youth, the
study of scriptures and other holy books aroused his interest and curiosity
about spiritual realization, but he had to endure many hardships before he
could attain inner knowledge. His poetry and *kafis* express that struggle and
have many references to Islamic thought and mystic literature. In time, he
became one of the great Sufi poets of the Punjab, and his verses have made
him popular among all religious communities. Scholars and dervishes have
called him "The Sheikh of Both the Worlds," "The Man of God," and
"The Knower of Spiritual Grace."

Bulleh Shah's longing for union with God made him search for a
renowned master—Hazrat Shah Inayat Qadiri, who appears in many of
the poet's *kafis* in the role of spiritual guide and savior. Bulleh Shah was a
sayyed—he could trace his ancestry directly to the Prophet Muhammad—
and many of his family and friends were critical of his devotion to Shah
Inayat, who came from a family of peasant farmers. Bulleh Shah opposed
such distinctions. He expressed his disdain for orthodox scholars and
chastised them in his verse for hypocrisy and for ignoring essence for form.

Every moment love's new surge of spring
When the ways of love-rapture I gained
Differences of me and you were not sustained
The shell and pith were washed clean, unstained
Wherever I look the friend is befriending
Every moment love's a new surge of spring.
  Bulleh Shah

Bulleh Shah was often known to be in a trance, a state of spiritual bliss attained through music and dancing. He denied being a either a devout worshiper or a blasphemer. Neither good nor evil, he is seeking the bliss of union with the Beloved:

> Bulleh who am I, what do I know?
> Neither in mosques an orthodox acolyte
> Nor in any blaspheming rite
> Nor pure amongst the defiled recondite
> Neither Moses am I, nor Pharaoh
> Bulleh who am I, what do I know?[30]

Due to a misunderstanding with Shah Inayat, the disciple and master became estranged. In another *kafi*, Bulleh Shah describes his pain at this rupture:

> He left me, and himself departed;
> What fault was there in me?
> Neither at night nor in the day do I sleep in peace
> My eyes pour out tears!
> Sharper than swords and spears are the arrows of love!
> There is no one as cruel as love;
> This malady no physician can cure.[31]

The master is aware at all times of the disciple. Expelling Bulleh from the fold was a way to test his resolve, to see that he would be fit to receive the invaluable wealth of the Word of God. When Shah Inayat realized that true repentance and separation had purified Bulleh, he welcomed him back as his disciple. The master embraced Bulleh and continued his teachings

عشق دی نویں نویں بہار

جاں میں رمز عشق دی پائی

مینا توتا مار گوائی

اندر باہر ہوئی صفائی

جتھوں ویکھاں یار و یار

بُلھے شاہ

245

with him. Bulleh felt that no distinction remained between the two, and in this *kafi* describes his state of merging in the master (*fana-fi'l-shaikh*):

> Repeating the name of Ranjha
> I have become Ranjha myself.
> Call ye me "Dhido-Ranjha,"
> Ranjha is in me, I am in Ranjha,
> no other thought exists in my mind.
> I am not, He alone is.[32]

When one arrives at this state of awareness, the illusion of duality disappears and the glory of the Beloved is seen everywhere. Bulleh Shah declares that love for the Lord has so radically changed him that his individual self—his ego—has been totally eliminated. He has now realized his true self, hidden behind the veil of the physical body. His identification with the Supreme Being has given him the grace of divine light.

> I have got lost in the city of love,
> I am being cleansed, withdrawing myself
> from my head, hands and feet.
> I have got rid of my ego, and have
> attained my goal.
> Thus it has all ended well.
> O Bulleh, the Lord pervades both the worlds;
> None now appears a stranger to me.[33]

Consumed with the love of God, Bulleh became the personification of compassion and forgiveness. He began to see the Divine in every being, and

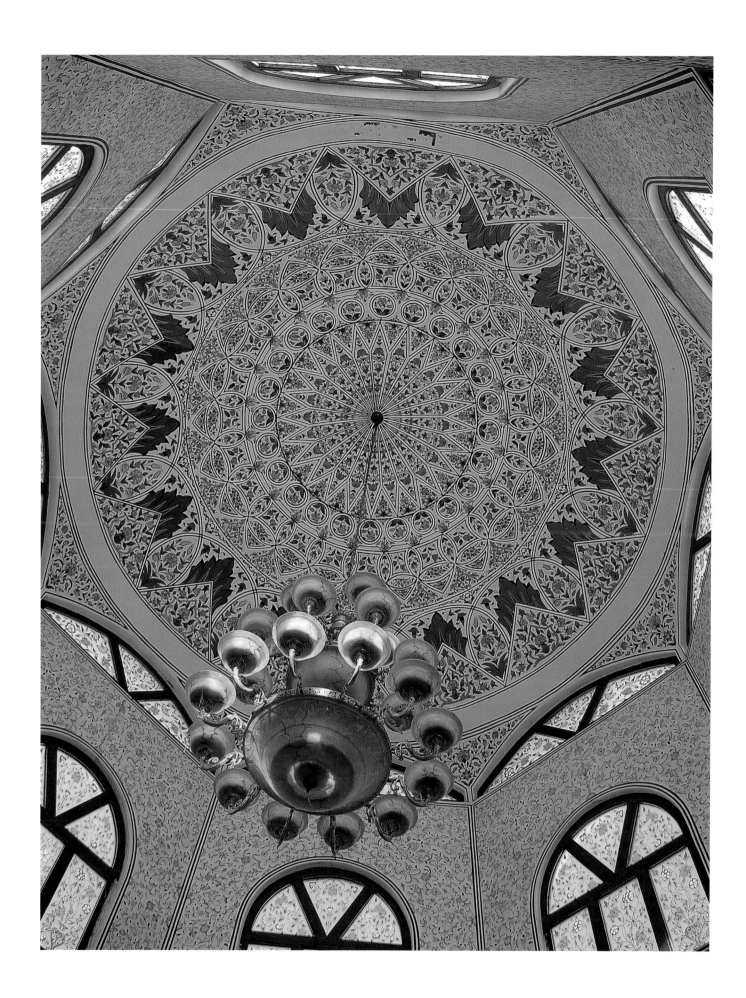

distinctions of caste and religion, friend and adversary, ceased to have any meaning for him.

An oft-told tale says that Bulleh Shah was engaged in meditation inside his chamber during the month of Ramadan while some of his disciples sat outside eating carrots. A group of orthodox Muslims who were keeping the fast happened to pass by. When they saw the disciples sitting at a *faqir*'s abode and violating the fast, they were enraged. They shouted angrily, "Are you not ashamed of eating in the month of Ramadan, and that also at the abode of a *faqir*?" The disciples replied, "Brother believers, continue on your way. We are feeling hungry. That is why we are eating."

When asked, "Who are you?" the disciples replied, "We are Muslims and we are hungry."

The visitors again commanded them to stop eating, but the disciples did not listen. So the visitors snatched the carrots from the hands of the disciples and threw them away. As they were about to leave, it struck them that the *faqir* of these impious people must have allowed such disrespect of Ramadan, so they turned back to ask him what kind of instruction he had given them. "Who are you? What do you teach?"

Bulleh, who was meditating with his eyes closed, raised his hands heavenward.

They asked him again, "Why don't you speak? Who are you?"

Bulleh once again raised his arms.

They took him to be a mad man and went away. Soon after they left, the disciples entered the chamber, complaining that they had been beaten. Bulleh told them that they must have provoked the believers. The disciples denied this. Bulleh said, "What did they ask you?" The disciples replied, "They asked us who we were, and we said we were Muslims."

Bulleh then replied, "That's why you were beaten. You professed to be something and you suffered. I didn't profess to be anything, and they said nothing to me. To consider oneself something emanates from the sense of ego. Such a person is still under the sway of *maya* (illusion), and has not had a vision of Truth so far. One who has had such a vision comes to know his true Self and gets liberated from the bondage of caste, religion, and country."

In Bulleh's Shah's shrine in Kasur a large open courtyard welcomes men and women equally and inspires musicians and dancers to demonstrate their devotion. A new shrine has been built over the simple old one, and it feels sadly alien to the spirit of Bulleh Shah and his teachings. The modern lines and marble tiles are out of place in this rural town. But a group of local musicians is playing and singing in the corner, under a tree. Soon the courtyard fills with people, and the cold new architecture is softened by the colorful garments and enthusiastic dancing of the crowd. Sharply fragrant green fenugreek, known as *kasuri methi*, is piled in huge stacks near the courtyard entrance. I buy a bundle from a farmer who recommends boiling it in water and drinking it as tea upon rising in the morning, as a way to cure all aches and pains.

My encounter with Bulleh Shah has been different from my other visits to the shrines. For me, Bulleh's spirit is not just in his shrine. It is in every village and on the lips of musicians throughout South Asia. Reading his passionate verses and listening to the music played with the sung *kafis* distills the experience of Bulleh Shah's ecstatic search for God. The listener can imagine his magnetic personality and his courage in flouting convention. In his work one finds poignancy, ardor, longing—and sincerity, sacrifice, and renunciation.

For me and thousands of others, the poems of Bulleh Shah demonstrate that the soul, like God, has no religion, no caste, no country. These distinctions are born out of time and space, but the soul is timeless and infinite.

> I take myself to be the beginning and the end;
> I do not recognize aught except the One.[34]

History has shaped the lives and beliefs of the Indus Valley's inhabitants. The pageant of many races, the varied hues and textures of many civilizations and cultures, have merged to form the unique soul of this land. And the place itself is still infused with the living traditions of poetry, philosophy, literature, and music of the Sufi shaikhs whose sacred spirit illuminates the land.

Notes

1. Ibn ʻArabi, *Divine Sayings,* 99.
2. Mir ʻAli Shir Qani, *Maklinama,* 11.
3. Schimmel, *Nightingales under the Snow,* 86.
4. Gidvani, *Shah Abdul Latif,* 47.
5. Subhan, *Sufism, Its Saints and Shrines,* 128.
6. Hujwírí, *The "Kashf al-Mahjub,"* 345.
7. Ibid., 30.
8. Iqbal, *The Secrets of the Self,* 95–96.
9. Dhaul, *The Sufi Shrine of Ajmer,* 25.
10. Hazrat Muinuddin Chishti, in Beqq, *Hazrat Muinuddin Chishti,* 12.
11. Schimmel, *Islam in the Indian Subcontinent,* 24.
12. Ernst and Lawrence, *Sufi Martyrs of Love,* 160.
13. Ibid., 161.
14. Awliya, *Morals for the Heart,* 33.
15. Ernst and Lawrence, 161.
16. Ibid., 35.
17. Niazi, *The Life and Works of Sultan Alauddin Khalji,* 125.
18. Ernst and Lawrence, 76.
19. Narang, "The Qawwali: An Indo-Islamic Cultural Fusion," 26.
20. Schimmel, *Mystical Dimensions of Islam,* 353.
21. Ibid., 212.
22. Carl W. Ernst, personal communication, 22 December 2007.
23. Cited in Chittick, *The Self-Disclosure of God,* 265.
24. Ghaffaar, *Masterworks of Punjabi Sufi Poetry: Shah Husayn: Within Reach,* 691.
25. Schimmel, "Poetic Visions of Lahore," in Quraeshi, *Lahore: The City Within,* 35.
26. Schimmel, *Islam in the Indian Subcontinent,* 98.
27. Schimmel, *Mystical Dimensions of Islam,* 362.
28. Rizvi, *A History of Sufism in India,* vol. 2, 38.
29. Ghaffaar, *Bulleh Shaah: Within Reach,* 176.
30. Ibid., 201.
31. Bulleh Shah, *Bulleh Shah: The Love-Intoxicated Iconoclast,* 235.
32. Ibid., 25.
33. Ibid., 26.
34. Ibid., 36.

THE SUFI IS IN NO NEED OF ANY HINT OR EXPLANATION
TO RECOGNIZE THE DIVINE TRUTH.
QAUL-I SUFIYA

Afterword

I began this exploration with recollections from a childhood in Pakistan, at a time when diverse communities flourished. Islam provided the firm ground in which locally inflected spiritual influences took root, and faith was a matter of personal choice, not of legislation or intimidation. When the British partitioned the Indian subcontinent in 1947, they created two separate and independent states, the Dominion of Pakistan and the Union of India.

Mohammad Ali Jinnah, the founder of Pakistan, famously declared to the peoples of his new country:

> You are free; you are free to go to your temples, you are free to go to your mosques or to any other place of worship in this State of Pakistan. You may belong to any religion or caste or creed—that has nothing to do with the business of the State. ... We are starting in the days where there is no discrimination, no distinction between one community and another, no discrimination between one caste or creed and another. We are starting with this fundamental principle that we are all citizens and equal citizens of one State.[1]

Jinnah's message was in keeping with the beliefs of the early Muslims who introduced Islam into the Indus Valley many centuries before. These followers of the Prophet were careful to stress that the new ideas would adhere only if they were practiced within the cultural traditions of the local people. Despite the early idealism of Pakistan's founders, the coexistence of different faiths eroded quickly. The concept of a separate homeland for the Muslims of the subcontinent had been percolating in the minds of the Muslim intelligentsia for decades, and in 1956 Pakistan was declared an Islamic republic. Islam was the glue that bound together the disparate ethnic groups that resided in the region. Now, however, ordinary people's lives are being disrupted by the encroaching dictums of groups like the Taliban, radical clerics, and the proliferation of *madrasahs* that teach a doctrine stripped of spiritual nuance.

My own journey to the Sufi shrines of the region was in part an attempt to understand how religious practice ramifies in unique ways in each social context: in distinct places where a particular form of worship has intersected with the infinite layers of a particular local culture. I found that the unity derived from a universal love for God continues to adapt to the contemporary spiritual and physical geography of this region, constantly reinventing what it means to practice the mystical dimensions of Islam while respecting the generational continuity of centuries of pilgrimage and ritual.

The sacred spaces I visited—shrines and meditation lodges throughout the Indus Valley—are places where a Sufi shaikh's mystical authority is articulated. People have created these sanctuaries as tributes, as symbolic expressions of their acknowledgment of the Divine. During my journey I also found places in nature that communicated divinity through their spectacular beauty. The local people were aware of the spiritual significance of these places and offered their prayers at architectural and natural sites alike. The magnetic power these sacred spaces exude inspires a sense of awe. Such shrines remind me how personal an experience the inner dimension of Sufism is. A shaikh's legacy is never fixed in the imagination. Different perceptions of the divine mystery are reflected in the changing realities and ever-evolving rites and practices through which the devout integrate the sacred teachings into contemporary experience.

Many schools of Qur'anic interpretation contend that an impenetrable gulf separates the individual and the Divine. Sufi thought advances a different view of a personal, mystical, and even romantic relationship between the believer and the Divine, the mystical Lover and Beloved. Ritual practice is more than superstition. It gives each pilgrim a point of entry into a personal relationship with the Divine. As I have traced the routes and rites of these spiritual pathways, my belief in the power of a specific, place-based worship has grown stronger than ever.

Narratives occupy a central position in Sufism in this part of the world. They are interwoven, told, and retold. Each generation reshapes the original narrative with memories based on their own perceptions and flavored by changing political realities. The central element holding these narrative networks together is the telling and retelling of stories: stories that affirm, reaffirm, and continually reshape the experiential dimensions of Sufi piety and identity.

For Sufis the principle of love is of primary importance. It is the foundation, the agent of creation, and the essence of God. It is the pursuit of love and the abandonment of reason that allow knowledge of God. This

passionate, all-consuming love is what gives a Sufi the strength to annihilate the ego and seek unity with the Divine.

Poetry and song are the languages of love. Both music and oral tradition are important to ritual practice in the Sufi tradition. They form a bridge between dream and reality, between chaos and order, and—in an artistic sense—between the mundane and the sublime. They are powerful tools in helping ordinary people understand that God created humans in the image of the Divine.

The sacred spaces of Sufism serve as the outward and public expression of saints' inner mystical journeys and knowledge. Through the preservation, commemoration, and celebration of sites associated with a given Sufi teacher, his disciples argue over, legitimate, perform, and display the religious authority of their beloved and heroic master.

Over long periods of time and great distances, Sufis developed rituals and practices in search of a direct pathway to God; like all mystics, they avoided the strictures of orthodoxy and organized religion. Today Sufis in Pakistan are being persecuted under the guise of the authoritarian ideals of extremist Islamists. Because the economic and political frustrations of the local populace are unanswered by the state, some people embrace the certainty of a creed that is prescriptive, that "guarantees" paradise, and that offers an instant community. When confronted with the choice between spiritual intangibles and the tangible rewards promised by martyrdom, the tangible may be difficult to resist. This is not because the spiritual aspects of Sufism are impotent or irrelevant. Rather, too many people no longer have access to such spiritual relief, expression, and inspiration. Music and dance are being banned or are not performed due to the threat of bombs and violence. Gathering at a shrine may be hazardous. Civil society erodes.

My journey was motivated by the belief that becoming a pilgrim might show me how to deconstruct the monolithic view of Islam. To gain true understanding, I will have to mine the depths of the Muslim faith. But I have learned that to put oneself in a receptive frame of mind, to allow intuition to flow, transforms one into a vessel for the Divine. Souls are the receptacles of God's message, and the heart is the vital center of existence. Relationship to God can be personal, not understood exclusively as a collective uniformity experienced among the entire *ummah*. The Prophet Muhammad's vision of tolerance and unity must not be replaced by hatred and discord. Just as there is no singular and cohesive West, there is no "Muslim world." We do not have to pit "good" Islam against "bad" Islam to resist the reductive view of our faith. We can instead celebrate the singularities immanent within a religion whose faithful span the globe.

The words of Jalaluddin Rumi, the great thirteenth-century poet of
Sufism, resonate today:

> What is to be done, O Moslems? For I do not recognize myself.
> I am neither Christian, nor Jew, nor Gabr, nor Moslem.
> I am not of the East, nor of the West, nor of the land, nor of the sea;
> I am not of nature's mint, nor of the circling heavens.
> I am not of the earth, nor of the water, nor of air, nor of fire;
> I am not of the empyrean, nor of the dust, nor of existence, nor of
> entity.
> I am not of India, nor of China, nor of Bulgaria, nor of Saqsin;
> I am not of the kingdom of Iraqain, nor of the country of Khorasan.
> I am not of this world, nor of the next, nor of Paradise, nor of Hell;
> I am not of Adam, nor of Eve, nor of Eden and Rizwan.
> My place is the Placeless, my trace is the Traceless;
> 'Tis neither body nor soul, for I belong to the soul of the Beloved.
> I have put duality away, I have seen that the two worlds are one;
> One I seek, One I know, One I see, One I call …[2]

I conclude with a renewed faith that spiritual journeys never end.
My questions have led to more questions, and there are no easy answers.
Indeed, the recurring images of the influences of the Sufis in this region,
their *silsilas*, routes, and pilgrimages, reinforce the fact that these mystical
dimensions are embedded in the nature of this people and this land. They
are transitory, and they are personal. Sacred space is within.

Notes

1. Mohammad Ali Jinnah, "Presidential Address to the Constituent
    Assembly of Pakistan at Karachi," 11 August 1947. http://pakistanspace.
    tripod.com/archives/47jin11.htm.
2. Chittick, *The Sufi Doctrine of Rumi*, 76.

GLOSSARY

ahl al-kitab: "People of the Book"; non-Muslims who have received scriptures attributed to God, including Jews and Christians

ahl al-suffa: "People of the Bench"; Medina ascetics given permission by Muhammad to live in a corner of the Medina mosque

ahl-i hazl: scoffers

ajrak: textile blockprinted in indigo, crimson, black, and yellow

Akhwan al-Safa: "Brotherhood of Purity"; authors of one of the most complete medieval encyclopedias of the sciences

al-Janna: "the garden"; Qur'anic term for Paradise

al-Fatawa al-Sufiya: "Decrees of the Sufis"

al-Hind: Arabic term for India

alif: first letter of Arabic alphabet; represents the word *Allah* (God)

Allah u Akbar, Allah u Akbar: "Allah is Great, Allah is Great"

arifeen: "those who have knowledge"

azan (adhan, azaan): Islamic call to prayer recited by the muezzin five times a day

ba: second letter in the Arabic alphabet

*bait*s: stanza or line of Arabic poetry, usually a couplet

baraka: "blessing"; spiritual grace issued from God, spiritual grace of shaikh

basti: shantytown

batin: "the hidden"; interior or hidden meaning of the Qur'an

bhit: "sand hill"

biryani: rice-based food of spices, vegetables, potatoes, and sometimes meat

Bismillah ur-rahman ur-rahim: "In the name of Allah the beneficent and merciful"

chadar: cloth laid on graves, stamped with religious sayings and embellished with calligraphy

chahar bagh: rectangular or square garden of four symmetrical sections; based on Qur'anic description of Paradise

chahar taq: "four arch" in Persian; pavilion of four walls with arches, topped by a hemispheric dome

chahar yar: "four friends"; probably originally applied to the first four caliphs (Abu Bakr, Umar ibn al-Khattab, Uthman ibn Affan, and Ali ibn Abi Talib); also used to refer to the lineage of Chishti saints: Hajji Uthman Harwani, Khwaja Muinuddin Chishti, Qutbuddin Bakhtiyar Kaki, and Fariduddin Ganj-i Shakar

charpoy: bed with a wooden frame around a web of loosely woven rope

Chishtiya: mystic order of Sufis in India and Pakistan

dargah: shrine built over the grave of a Muslim saint, includes mosque, meeting rooms, schools, hospitals, and residences; "portal"

degh-walas: "street of cauldrons"

Deoband: Sunni Muslim revivalist movement developed as a reaction to British colonialism in India

dervish: Sufi Muslim ascetic who practices extreme poverty to learn humility

dhamal: Sufi dance

Din-i-Ilahi: "Divine Faith" in Persian; a syncretist religious doctrine founded by Mughal Emperor Akbar

divan: a bundle of written sheets, a small book, or a collection of poems; also an Oriental council of state or its chief officer

dupatta: scarf worn over woman's shoulders and/or head

fana-fi'l-shaikh: extinction of self in one's master

faqir: ascetic wanderer

fatiha: first chapter of the Qur'an, often used as a devotional prayer

ghalibkari or *qalabkari*: a lattice or network of ribs in stucco plaster or brick masonry

girah: "knot"; knotted geometric patterns of lines woven into nets or webs

hadith: oral traditions relating to words and deeds of the Prophet Muhammad

hadith qudsi: oral tradition of the words of God as expressed by Muhammad

hafiz: "guardian"; someone who has memorized the Qur'an

hajj: pilgrimage to holy city of Mecca; Fifth Pillar of Islam

hasht bihisht: "Eight Paradises" (Persian); floor plan with eight outer chambers surrounding a central room; basis for many Islamic buildings

hawa: "air" or "winds"; in design the term refers to the subtleties of form

hazrat: the spiritual presence of a saint; also an honorific

hijri: Islamic calendar (*anno Hegirae*: AH; before Hijra: BH)

Hindawi (also Hindvi): "Indian language"; mother language of modern Hindi and Urdu

imam: male religious authority who leads prayers in a mosque

insan e kamil: "a perfect man"; perfected or completed human being; also used as an honorific title for Muhammad

islam: literally, "submission"; also "peace"

jihad: struggle to improve self and society

jihadi: one who participates in a *jihad*

kafi: classical Sindhi and Punjabi Sufi poetry

kalasha: finial of the Hindu *shikhara,* or temple spire

kalima: "the phrase"; First Pillar of Islam, primary declaration of faith: "There is no God but Allah. Muhammad is His Messenger."

kameez: traditional long tunic

kankar or *kasuri chuna*: a naturally occurring hydraulic lime (calcium carbonate) found in the shape of spongelike nodules

Kashf al-Mahjub: "The Unveiling of the Hidden," one of the first Persian treatises on the mystical life, written by Data Ganj Bakhsh

kashikari: art of glazed tile mosaics decorated with calligraphy or graphic designs

kasuri methi: fenugreek plant, used as an herb and a seasoning *kazi* (or *qadi*): judge or magistrate ruling by *sharia* over all legal matters involving Muslims

khadim: "caretaker"; custodian of mosque or shrine

khalifah: "successor," ruler of a Muslim community; caliph

khanqah: building designed for a Sufi brotherhood; place of spiritual retreat like a hospice or seminary

khwab-i ghaflat: "the sleep of negligence"

kikar: "the sweet thorn"; a small, thorny acacia tree

Kufic: oldest calligraphic form of Arabic

kurta: loose unisex shirt falling near knees

lal: "garnet" or "ruby" in Punjabi; "red" in Hindustani

lakh: one hundred thousand (100,000); Indian numbering system unit

langar: free food distributed to poor at *dargah/khanqah*

langar-khana: kitchen where *langar* is prepared and distributed to poor

La ilaha illah hoo: "There is no God but He"

maasi: "auntie" in Hindi and other Indian languages

madrasah: Arabic for any type of educational institution

Mahbub-i-Ilahi: Beloved of God; a name of Nizamuddin Auliya

Majma al-Akhbar: "Collected News"; collected sayings of Rukn-i-Alam, compiled by his followers

majzub: "divinely intoxicated"

makhdum: title for descendant of a Sufi master (shaikh)

malfuzat: teachings and sayings of a Sufi shaikh

mandala: geometric design symbolizing the universe, used in Hinduism and Buddhism as a meditation aid

mannat: "wish" in Punjabi

maqam: "place of residence" or "station" in Arabic; a spiritual stage on the Sufi Path to vision of and union with God

masnawi: couplets in rhymed pairs, typical of Persian verse and used for epic and didactic poetry

maujbah: inverted lotus shape on a Hindu temple spire

maulvi: honorific Islamic title for religious scholar

maya: "illusion" in Sanskrit; philosophical concept of a powerful force that creates the illusion that the world is real

mihrab: niche in mosque indicating Mecca's direction

mithai: Indian sweets made mainly of sugar and milk

mochi gali: "street of the cobblers"

mu'mineen: "those who believe"

Mughals: a Muslim dynasty that ruled most of northern India, CE 1526–1707

muhajirs: Urdu-speaking Indian immigrant community in Pakistan

mullah: Muslim religious scholar; Muslim title denoting "lord"; "protector" (*mawla*) in Arabic

muqarnas: type of decorative corbel used in traditional Islamic and Persian architecture

muqarribeen: "those who are the nearest" to God

murid: "committed one" in Arabic; one who has committed to a teacher in the spiritual path of Sufism

mutawalis: pious followers who regulate the various rituals at the shrine

naan: unleavened Indian bread

naat: poetry that specifically praises the Prophet Muhammad

nafs: the self, and in Sufism, the false ego

nafs-i-ammara: "The Commanding Lower-Self" (Qur'an 12:53); the self that is attracted to the material world and its evils

nafs-i-mutmainna: "The Soul at Peace" (Qur'an 89:27); the self that is faithful and without materialism or worldly problems

naqqashi: fresco

nawab: Mughal viceroy

nazr: gifts of food or valuables that are blessed and then distributed to the poor

padma: lotus symbolizing divine purity and enlightenment in Hindu mythology

paan: betel leaf with areca nut used as a palate cleanser and breath freshener

pirs: shaikhs

pukka kali: fine lime

qafila: caravan

qaul: "utterance" in Arabic

qawwal: one who provides choral support in a *qawwali* performance by repeating key verses and refrains in rhythms of increasing intensity

qawwali: devotional Sufi singing

Qur'an: the central religious text of Islam, considered by Muslims to be the final revelation of God

qutb: "pole star" or "axis" in Arabic

raga: in classical Indian, Bangladeshi, and Pakistani music, a melodic framework based on a particular musical scale

rawda or *rauza*: "garden," specifically, garden of Paradise

roti: unleavened flatbread

sajjada or *sajjada-nashin*: descendant of shaikh or of disciple of shaikh, one who tends to the *dargah* erected over shaikh's tomb and inaugurates annual *urs* festival

Sakinat al-Awliya: "The Peace of the Saints"

salat: Second Pillar of Islam; formal prayer of Islam performed five times a day

sama: musical Sufi ritual of prayer, song, and dance

sarangi: short-necked fiddle used in South Asian music

sarmast: "intoxicated one"

sayyed: male descendant of the Prophet Muhammad

shah: Persian term for leader

Shah jo Rag: intricate musical pieces sung in falsetto that are said to have curative powers

shaikh: "elder" in Arabic, also known as *pir* and *khwaja*; in Sufism, an authority learned in religion; in Sufi orders, an honorific for an elder Sufi authority who teaches, initiates, and guides

shalwar: loose-fitting trousers usually worn with *kameez*

shamsa: solar motif

sharia: religious law of Islam

shikhara: tower or spire above sanctuary or temple

shirk: idolatry

silsila: "chain" in Arabic; succession or lineage of education from master to student

sitar: stringed instrument of lute family

sulh-i-kull: "peace with all" or "universal peace"

sura: chapter in the Qur'an, of which there are 114

surs: song chapters

tabla: pair of small drums of different pitch used in Hindustani music of northern India

tamboro: stringed musical instrument invented by Shah Abdul Latif

tang: cotton pajamas

tariqa: "road" in Arabic; Muslim spiritual path toward direct knowledge of God or Reality

tazakari: imitation brick

thoba: stone carving, stone inlay

Tughluq: dynasty in northern India, CE 1321–1398

ulema: religious teacher of Islamic community

ummah: "community, nation" in Arabic; entire Muslim world or diaspora

urs: "wedding" in Arabic; death anniversary of Sufi shaikh, celebrated at saint's *dargah*

virahini: loving or yearning woman

wahdat al-wujud: "The Unity of Being" in Arabic; Sufi philosophy emphasizing oneness with and of God; Muhyiuddin ibn al-Arabi was its major proponent

wali: "saint" in Arabic; in Sufism, denotes friend of God; can also mean Muslim mystics

waqf: inalienable religious endowment of building or plot of land for Muslim religious or charitable purposes

wissal: meeting of lover and the Beloved; "union," the ultimate goal of the Sufi

yantra: "to restrain, curb, check" in Sanskrit; symbol, diagram, or geometric figure used in Buddhist and Eastern mysticism for meditation and spiritual contemplation

yogi: male practitioner of meditative practices in Buddhism and Hinduism

zahir: apparent meaning, or normal human interpretation, of the Qur'an

zakat: Third Pillar of Islam, the giving of a small percentage of one's income to charity

zarb: pulse or beat of music and poetry

zikr: "remembrance, invocation" in Arabic; Islamic devotional act involving continual repeated recitation of the names of God

BIBLIOGRAPHY

Advani, Kalyar. *Sachal*. New Delhi: Sahitya Academy, 1971.

Allana, Ghulam Ali. *Four Classical Poets of Sind: Minyom Shah Inat, Shah Abdul Latif, Sachal Sarmast, Sami*. Karachi: Institute of Sindhology, 1983.

Armstrong, Karen. *Muhammad: A Biography of the Prophet*. San Francisco: Harper San Francisco, 1992.

Asani, Ali Sultaan Ali. *Celebrating Muhammad: Images of the Prophet in Popular Muslim Poetry*. Columbia, SC: University of South Carolina Press, 1995.

—. "Propagating the Message: Popular Sufi Songs and Spiritual Transformation in South Asia," *Bulletin of the Henry Martyn Institute of Islamic Studies,* vol. 15, nos. 3–4, 1996, 5–15.

Aslan, Reza. *No God but God: The Origins, Evolution, and Future of Islam*. New York: Random House, 2005.

Awliya, Nizam ad-Din. *Morals for the Heart*. New York: Paulist Press, 1992.

Beqq, William. *The Holy Biography of Hazrat Muinuddin Chishti*. The Hague: East-West Publications, 1977.

Burckhardt, Titus. *An Introduction to Sufi Doctrine*. Lahore: Sh. M. Ashraf, 1959.

Chittick, William C. *The Vision of Islam*. St. Paul, MN: Paragon House, 1994.

—. *The Self-Disclosure of God: Principles of Ibn al-'Arabi's Cosmology*. Albany: SUNY Press, 1998.

—. *Imaginal Worlds, Ibn al-'Arabi, and the Problem of Religious Diversity*. Lahore: Sohail Academy, 2001.

—. *The Sufi Doctrine of Rumi*. Bloomington, IN: World Wisdom, Inc., 2005.

Critchlow, Keith. *Islamic Patterns: An Analytical and Cosmological Approach*. New York: Schocken Books, 1976.

Dhaul, Laxmi. *The Sufi Saint of Ajmer*. Mumbai: Thea Enterprises, 2001.

—. *The Sufi Shrine of Ajmer*. New Delhi: Rupa & Co., 2004.

Eaton, Richard. "Sufi Folk Literature and the Expansion of Islam," *History of Religions*, vol. 14, no. 2, 1974–75.

—. *Sufis of Bijapur, 1300–1700*. Princeton, NJ: Princeton University Press, 1978.

Elias, Jamal. *Death before Dying: The Sufi Poems of Sultan Bahu*. Berkeley and Los Angeles: University of California Press, 1998.

Ernst, Carl W. *Sufism*. Boston: Shambhala South Asian Editions, 1997.

—. *Following Muhammad: Rethinking Islam in the Contemporary World*. Chapel Hill, NC: University of North Carolina Press, 2003.

—. *Eternal Garden: Mysticism, History, and Politics at a South Asian Sufi Center*, 2nd ed. New Delhi: Oxford University Press, 2005.

Ernst, Carl W., trans. "India as a Sacred Islamic Land," in *Religions of India in Practice*, ed. Donald S. Lopez, Jr. Princeton: Princeton University Press, 1993, 556–564.

Ernst, Carl W., and Bruce B. Lawrence. *Sufi Martyrs of Love: The Chishti Order in South Asia and Beyond*. New York: Palgrave Macmillan, 2002.

Fazal, Abul. *A'een e Akbari*, vol. 1, *A'een 35—tasveerkhana*. Urdu translation by Maulvi Muhammad Fida Ali. Lahore: Sang-e-Meel Publications, 1988.

Ghaffaar, Muzaffar A. *Masterworks of Punjabi Sufi Poetry: Bulleh Shaah: Within Reach*, vol. 2. Lahore: Ferozsons, 2005.

—. *Masterworks of Punjabi Sufi Poetry: Shah Husayn: Within Reach*. Lahore: Cyril Sons Ltd., 2005.

Gidvani, M. M. *Shah Abdul Latif*. London: The India Society, 1922.

Haeri, Muneera. *The Chishtis: A Living Light*. Oxford: Oxford University Press, 2000.

Hafiz. *The Gift: Poems by the Great Sufi Master*, trans. Daniel Ladinsky. New York: Arkana, 1999.

Hanif, N. *Biographical Encyclopedia of Sufis: South Asia*. New Delhi: Sarup & Sons, 2000.

Helminski, Camille Adams. *The Women of Sufism: A Hidden Treasure: Writings and Stories of Mystic Poets, Scholars, and Saints*. Boston: Shambhala Publications, 2003.

Hujwiri, 'Ali ibn 'Uthman al-. *The "Kashf al-Mahjub," the Oldest Persian Treatise on Sufism by al-Hujwiri*, trans. Reynold A. Nicholson. Lahore: Islamic Book Foundation, 1976.

Ibn 'Arabi, Muhyiuddin. *Divine Sayings: 101 Hadith Qudsi: The Mishkat al-Anwar of Ibn 'Arabi,* trans. Stephen Hirtenstein and Martin Notcutt. Oxford: Anqa Publishing, 2008.

Ibn Battuta. *Travels in Asia and Africa 1325–1354*, trans. H. A. R. Gibb. New York: Robert M. McBride & Company, 1929.

Iqbal, Sheikh Muhammad. *The Secrets of the Self (Asrar-i Khudi)*, trans. Reynold A. Nicholson. Lahore: Farhan Publishers, 1977.

Jotwani, Motilal. *Shah Abdul Latif: His Life and Work*. Delhi: University of Delhi, 1975.

Lawrence, Bruce B. *Notes from a Distant Flute: The Extant Literature of Pre-Mughal Indian Sufism*. Boston: Shambhala Publications, 1979.

—. "The Eastward Journey of Muslim Kingship," in *The Oxford History of Islam*, ed. John L. Esposito. Oxford: Oxford University Press, 1995, 395–432.

—. "Islam in South Asia," in *The Oxford Encyclopedia of the Modern Islamic World*, ed. John L. Esposito. Oxford: Oxford University Press, 1999, 278–284.

Lings, Martin. *What Is Sufism?* Berkeley: University of California Press, 1975.

—. "The Seven Deadly Sins in the Light of the Symbolism of Number," in *The Sword of Gnosis: Metaphysics, Cosmology, Tradition, Symbolism*, ed. Jacob Needleman. London: Arkana, 1986, 218–219.

—. *Symbol and Archetype: A Study of the Meaning of Existence*. Cambridge, MA: Quinta Essentia, 1991.

—. *Sufi Poems: A Medieval Anthology*. Cambridge: Islamic Texts Society, 2004.

Michon, Jean-Louis. *Lights of Islam: Institutions, Culture, Arts, and Spirituality in the Islamic City*. Islamabad: Lok Virsa, 2000.

Michon, Jean-Louis, and Roger Gaetani, eds. *Sufism: Love and Wisdom*, Bloomington, IN: World Wisdom, 2006.

Mir 'Ali Shir Qani'. *Maklinamah*, ed. Sayyid Hussamuddin Rashdi. Hyderabad: Sindi-i Adabi-i Burd, 1967.

Mumtaz, Kamil Khan. *Contemporary Architecture in Pakistan*. Karachi: Oxford University Press, 1999.

—. *Modernity and Tradition*. Karachi: Oxford University Press, 1999.

Narang, Gopi Chand. "The Qawwali: An Indo-Islamic Cultural Fusion," *HU: The Sufi Way*, April (2007), 20–26.

Nasr, Seyed Hossein. *Islamic Art and Spirituality*. Albany: State University of New York Press, 1987.

Niazi, Ghulam Sarwar Khan. *The Life and Works of Sultan Alauddin Khalji*. New Delhi: Atlantic Publishers & Distributors, 1992.

Nizami, Khaliq Ahmad. "Malfuzat ki tarikhi aham-miyat," in *Arshi Presentation Volume*, ed. Malik Ram. Delhi, 1961.

—. *Some Aspects of Religion and Politics in India during the 13th Century*. Bombay: Idarah-i Adabiyat-i Delli, 1961.

—. "Naqshbandi Influence on Mughal Rulers and Politics," *Islamic Culture* 39 (1965).

Quraeshi, Samina. *Lahore: The City Within*. Singapore: Concept Media Pte Ltd., 1988.

—. *Legacy of the Indus: A Discovery of Pakistan*. New York: Weatherhill, 1974.

Quraeshi, Samina, Annemarie Schimmel, and Ali Sultaan Ali Asani. *Legends of the Indus*. London: Asia Ink, 2004.

Qureshi, Regula Burckhardt. *Sufi Music of India and Pakistan: Sound, Context and Meaning in Qawwali*. Chicago: University of Chicago Press, 1995.

Rafat, Taufiq. *Bulleh Shah: A Selection*. Lahore: Vanguard Publications, 1982.

Rama Krishna, Lajwanti. *Punjabi Sufi Poets AD 1460–1900*. Karachi: Indus Publication, 1977 reprint.

Rizvi, Saiyid Athar Abbas. *A History of Sufism in India*, vol. 1: *Early Sufism and Its History in India to AD 1600*. Lahore: Suhail Academy, 2004.

—. *A History of Sufism in India*, vol. 2: *From Sixteenth Century to Modern Century*. Lahore: Suhail Academy, 2004.

Robinson, Francis. *Islam and Muslim History in South Asia*. New York: Oxford University Press, 2000.

Rumi, Jalal al-Din. *The Essential Rumi*, trans. Coleman Barks. San Francisco: Harper, 1995.

—. *The Illuminated Rumi*, trans. Coleman Barks. New York: Broadway Books, 1997.

—. *The Illustrated Rumi: A Treasury of Wisdom from the Poet of the Soul: A New Translation*, trans. Philip Dunn, Manuel Dunn Mascetti, and Reynolds A. Nicholson. San Francisco: Harper San Francisco, 2000.

Schimmel, Annemarie. *Mystical Dimensions of Islam*. Chapel Hill: University of North Carolina Press, 1975.

—. *Islam in the Indian Subcontinent*, Handbuch der Orientalistik, Zweite Abteilung: Indien 4:3. Leiden-Köln: E. J. Brill, 1980.

—. *As Through a Veil: Mystical Poetry in Islam*. New York: Columbia University Press, 1982.

—. *And Muhammad Is His Prophet*. Chapel Hill, University of North Carolina Press, 1985.

—. *The Triumphal Sun: A Study of the Works of Jaloddin Rumi*. Albany, NY: State University of New York Press, 1993.

—. *Nightingales under the Snow*. London: Khaniqahi Nimatullahi Publications, 1995.

—. *My Soul Is a Woman: The Feminine in Islam*. New York: Continuum Press, 1997.

—. *Islam in the Indian Subcontinent*. Lahore: Sang-e-Meel Publications, 2003.

—. *The Empire of the Great Mughals: History, Art and Culture*. New Delhi: Oxford University Press, 2005.

Shah, Bulleh. *Bulleh Shah: The Love-Intoxicated Iconoclast*, trans. J. R. Puri and Tilaka Raja Shagari. Punjab: Radha Soami Satsang Beas, 1986.

Shikoh, Dara. *Hasanat ul-'Arifin*, in *Dara Shikoh Life and Works*, trans. Bikrama Jit Hasrat. New Delhi: Munshiram Manoharlal, 1982, 11.

Sikand, Yoginder. "Madho Lal Hussain of Lahore: Beyond Hindu and Muslim," *Pakistan Christian Post*, October 31, 2005.

Sorley, H. T. *Shah Abdul Latif of Bhit: His Poetry, Life and Times*. Lahore, Karachi, and Dacca: Oxford University Press, 1966.

Stoddart, William. *Sufism: The Mystical Doctrines and Methods of Islam*. Wellingborough: Thorsons, 1976.

Subhan, John A. *Sufism, Its Saints and Shrines: An Introduction to the Study of Sufism with Special Reference to India and Pakistan*. Lucknow: Lucknow Pub. House, 1960.

Zhukovsky, Sidney Jerrold, and E. Denison Ross. *Bulletin of the School of Oriental Studies, University of London*, vol. 5, no. 3. Cambridge: Cambridge University Press, 1929.

Zweig, Connie. *A Moth to the Flame: The Life of the Sufi Poet Rumi*. Lanham, MD: Rowman & Littlefield Publishers, 2006.

CONTRIBUTORS

Ali S. Asani is Professor of Indo-Muslim and Islamic Religion and Cultures at Harvard University, where he teaches courses on Islam, Islamic Mysticism, Islam and the Arts, Islam in South Asia, and Urdu Language and Literature. He currently directs the university's Ph.D. program in Indo-Muslim Culture. His books include *The Bujh Niranjan: An Ismaili Mystical Poem* and *Ecstasy and Enlightenment: The Ismaili Literature of South Asia*. Professor Asani has been particularly active post–September 11 in improving the understanding of Islam and its role in Muslim societies.

Carl W. Ernst is a specialist in Islamic studies with a focus on West and South Asia. His published research, based on the study of Arabic, Persian, and Urdu, has been mainly devoted to the study of Islam and Sufism. His most recent book, *Following Muhammad: Rethinking Islam in the Contemporary World,* has received several international awards. He is the William R. Kenan, Jr., Distinguished Professor in the Department of Religious Studies and Director of the Carolina Center for the Study of the Middle East and Muslim Civilizations at the University of North Carolina at Chapel Hill.

Kamil Khan Mumtaz is a leading Pakistani architect and a founding member of the Lahore Conservation Society. As an architect, educator, author, and pioneer in the movement for the conservation of architectural heritage, Mr. Mumtaz has been influential in raising standards of architectural design in Pakistan and in the search for a contemporary architecture that is responsive to local climate, economy, and materials and is rooted in the indigenous culture. His publications include *Architecture in Pakistan* and *Modernity and Tradition*.

Samina Quraeshi is an award-winning educator, designer, artist, photographer, and author. She has devoted her life to cultivating the vital connections between cultural production, community, and communication and to bringing the multifaceted story of Islamic culture in South Asia to the world stage. She was formerly Henry R. Luce Professor in Family and Community at the University of Miami and Director of Design for the National Endowment for the Arts. She is currently the first Gardner Visiting Artist at the Peabody Museum, Harvard University. Ms. Quraeshi has exhibited her artwork internationally and is the author of *Legacy of the Indus: A Discovery of Pakistan, Lahore: The City Within,* and *Legends of the Indus*.

Acknowledgments

This book chronicles a journey that began many decades ago. Along the way, I have met fellow travelers who added to my knowledge and enhanced this work. The final product is the result of a rich and productive collaboration with many generous friends, relatives, colleagues, and mentors. If this work holds merit, it is because of their contributions. The flaws, omissions, and imperfections are mine.

In my work as an artist and educator I have used the lens of art and culture to reflect the cultural riches of the world in which I grew up. Over the past few years, I have been reappraising both my work and that world, and beliefs I long took for granted have been changing. Many of these shifts are profound. This book is a personal sketch, a broad-brush view based on the theme of Sufism in Pakistan and India, enriched by the poems, stories, and songs I have known and loved. It is also the fruit of the efforts of colleagues, friends, and members of my family, to whom I owe a great deal for helping me to grow and complete this book.

I am enormously grateful for the generosity of the Asian Cultural Council and the Gardner Fellowship at the Peabody Museum for the grants that allowed me to complete this book. Shahid Rafi opened many doors for me, and his enthusiasm for this endeavor allowed this dream to be realized. Collaborating with Mary McWilliams, Kimberly Mastellar, and Sunil Sharma at the Sackler Museum and Joseph Garver at the Harvard Map Collection taught me about mystical encounters throughout history. Nadeem Asghar, Naheed Rizvi, Humera Alam, and Uzma Usmani at the Lahore Museum allowed me access to their collections to find many of the images that illustrate this journey. Those images illuminate this text.

This manuscript has evolved thanks to the valuable suggestions of many readers. I am particularly grateful to Sher Ali Tareen who took time from his doctoral work to assist me with writing and research. His help in the initial stages of this project has been invaluable, and I could not have progressed without his assistance at a critical juncture. Ali Asani, Carl Ernst, and Kamil Khan Mumtaz have been instrumental in shaping the content of this book through their insight and knowledge of the subject. I will always value their friendship and their wisdom.

I thank Rosie Lee, who shared her knowledge and time through many stages and countless hours in conversations, adding her wit and critical eye. Milo Beach, Richard Meadow, Sunil Sharma, Aliya Iqbal, and Frank Korom directed me toward more research, and their comments have enriched the narrative as well. I thank Najm Hosain Syed and Muzaffar A. Ghaffar for introducing me to Punjabi poetry, and Najam Hussain for his generous help with finding field recordings of Sufi music.

At the Peabody Museum, William L. Fash, William and Muriel Seabury Howells Director, enthusiastically supported this challenging endeavor from its inception. Events and programs related to the "Sacred Spaces" project were expertly planned and executed by Pamela Gerardi. Ilisa Barbash, Sam Tager, Sarah Otto, and Daniel Ellis worked tirelessly to create a successful exhibition of the work.

This book would not have been possible without the skill, patience, and fortitude of Joan K. O'Donnell and Donna Dickerson, my ace team at the Peabody Museum Press. As editor, Joan worked tirelessly to help me sew myriad fragments of text and image into a book and accompanied me to India to oversee the final intensive production stages at Mapin Publishing. Donna organized the huge number of graphics files for production. I am also grateful to the intelligent energy of the interns who have assisted me during this process, Jennifer Z. Gong and Iram Nadroo.

I was fortunate to benefit from the design talents of Elizabeth Eddins, who worked with me to design early drafts of the book. Jamie Jett Walker came to my aid in preparing and refining design and image files for transmission to the Peabody. Kathryn Boulter and Emily Thornton were pivotal in organizing this material, and their curiosity and patience continually rescued this project from chaos. Devon Riley assiduously forged ahead and continued the process until we could envision the final form.

At Mapin Publishing, Amit Kharsani worked closely with me to realize the design, with the assistance of Gopal Limbad. Editors Carmen Kagal and Vinutha Mallya assisted in final preparations and proofing of the text. Bipin Shah's publishing acumen and fastidious attention to detail made the book a reality.

At Harvard University Press, I thank Sara Davis and Paul Adams for their enthusiasm about marketing the finished product. I also want to express my appreciation to Saleem Hussain of Liberty Books for representing the book in Pakistan.

Rachel Cooper, Director of Cultural Programs at the Asia Society, lent her invaluable collaborative spirit to this project, as did Richard Lanier and Ralph Samuelson of the Asian Cultural Council and Zeyba Rahman, who advised me on poetry and music.

The talented artists and photographers who accompanied me on this journey added their images to mine and made the narrative come alive. Taimoor Khan Mumtaz encouraged me to present the sacred art of calligraphy through the work of living masters and made it possible for me to work with Ustad Gauhar Qalam, Irfan Qureshi, Ghulam Murtaza, and Khurshid Raqam, who contributed the graceful and elegant calligraphy that ornaments this book. Ustad Gauhar Qalam was particulary open-hearted in supporting this project and sharing his very special art. I want to thank photographer Andreas Burgess for his help with the Nizamuddin segment (and so much more), Hafeez and Usman Mir for the sections on Hujwiri and Shah Husain, Shireen and Zaibun Pasha for their expertise in Lahore, Abid Ahsan for images of Multan and Bulleh Shah, Farooq Beg at Serendip Productions for the video still frames that are the basis for some of my photo montages, and Kamil Khan Mumtaz and Richard Shepard for the documentation of so many shrines and landscapes over the years. These collaborations and contributions have added life, beauty, and color.

Without the hospitality and nurturing of friends who supported me during this endeavor, my resolve would have faltered. In Pakistan, I would like to thank Khawar Mumtaz, Abida Hussain, Maneezeh Malik, Hamid Akhund, Maingul Aurangzeb, Adnan and Zainab Aurangzeb, Nariman and Franey Irani, and Maheen and Shahid Khan, each of whom generously welcomed this traveler home. In India, Mrinalini Sarabhai and Rajshree Sarabhai created a haven for me in their home and made me feel part of their wonderful family. Jasbir Singh provided friendship and counsel. In Cambridge, Robert Gardner and Adele Pressman offered critical feedback and unstinting friendship. In New York, Boston, Miami, London, and beyond, I would like to thank Julia Walker, Jay Keith, Christel Phipps, Kyra Montagu, Ellie Heydock, Bashan Rafique, and Mana and Shyama Sarabhai.

The encouragement of my family, the Shepards and the Quraeshis, has sustained me throughout this journey. The Quraeshi family, particularly Shams Bhai, Sohail, and Aniqah Quraeshi, continue their kind support. The ceaseless help and advice of my husband, Richard Shepard, and his unwavering belief in me sustain and nourish my wayward spirit. My children, Sadia and Cassim Shepard, offered themselves as critics and collaborators; their commitment to excellence and detail enriches this work. Without their talent, help, and love, I would have found this task impossible.

Finally, this book represents the lessons of many teachers I have had the good fortune to encounter over the years. Stories told with gestures and dramatic effects, listeners who added their own contributions, and narratives embroidered by experiences both real and imagined, these are all part of the oral tradition that is the connective thread of this work. The great Sufi shaikhs of South Asia have left us many teachings to enrich and enlighten our lives. I am indebted to their legacy and continue to be inspired by their visions.

Samina Quraeshi
South Dartmouth, Massachusetts
August 2009

This book is published in conjunction with the exhibition "Sacred Spaces: Reflections on a Sufi Path," held from 22 October 2009 to 30 April 2010 at the Peabody Museum of Archaeology and Ethnology, Harvard University, Cambridge, Massachusetts.

Annemarie Schimmel's poetry is used with the kind permission of Ali S. Asani and the Estate of Annemarie Schimmel.

Peabody Museum Press
Peabody Museum of Archaeology and Ethnology
Harvard University
11 Divinity Avenue
Cambridge, Massachusetts 02138 USA
T: 617-495-4255 • F: 617-495-7535
peapub@fas.harvard.edu • www.peabody.harvard.edu/publications

Mapin Publishing
502 Paritosh
Next to Darpana Academy of Performing Arts, Usmanpura Riverside
Ahmedabad 380013 India
T: 91 79 40 228 228 • F: 91 79 40 228 201
mapin@mapinpub.com • www.mapinpub.com

ISBN: 978-0-87365-859-1 (Peabody)
ISBN: 978-81-89995-31-7 (Mapin)

Library of Congress Cataloging-in-Publication Data

Quraeshi, Samina.
   Sacred spaces : a journey with the Sufis of the Indus / Samina Quraeshi ; with contributions by Ali S. Asani, Carl W. Ernst, Kamil Khan Mumtaz.
       p. cm.
   Published in conjunction with the exhibition "Sacred Spaces: Reflections on a Sufi Path," held from 22 October 2009 to 30 April 2010 at the Peabody Museum of Archaeology and Ethnology, Harvard University, Cambridge, Massachusetts.
   Includes bibliographical references.
   ISBN 978-0-87365-859-1 (cloth : alk. paper)
   1. Sufism—South Asia. 2. Sufis—South Asia. I. Asani, Ali S. (Ali Sultaan), 1954- II. Ernst, Carl W., 1950- III. Mumtaz, Kamil Khan. IV. Title.
   BP188.8.S64Q73 2010
   297.40954—dc22

                    2009029818

Editorial direction by Joan K. O'Donnell / Peabody Museum Press
Designed by Samina Quraeshi and Amit Kharsani
Copyedited by Joan K. O'Donnell / Peabody Museum Press and Carmen Kagal / Mapin Editorial
Jacket illustration © Andreas Burgess

Printed and bound in Singapore by Tien-Wah Press.
Printed on acid-free paper.

Picture Credits

All photographs and montages are by Samina Quraeshi except as listed. All images in this volume are copyright Samina Quraeshi except where other copyright notices appear below.

Abid Ahsan: 88–89, 128 bottom, 131, 190, 194–195, 197, 218–219, 224, 230–231, 233, 235, 237, 244–245, 250–251, 254–255, 257, 261

Abid Ahsan & Samina Quraeshi: 198–199

Abid Ahsan, Shireen Pasha, and Samina Quraeshi: 206–207, 216–217, 234

© Andreas Burgess: Jacket illustration, 12, 96–97, 100–101, 166, 170–171, 176–177, 178–179, 180–181, 182–183, 184–185

Courtesy Harvard Art Museum, Arthur M. Sackler Museum, Gift of Grenville L. Winthrop, Class of 1886, 1937.19; photo by David Mathews © President and Fellows of Harvard College: viii

Courtesy Harvard Art Museum, Arthur M. Sackler Museum, Gift of John Goelet, 1958.23; photo by Katya Kallsen © President and Fellows of Harvard College: 10

Courtesy Harvard Art Museum, Arthur M. Sackler Museum, Gift of John Goelet, 1958.242; photo by Allan Macintyre © President and Fellows of Harvard College: 20

Courtesy Harvard Art Museum, Arthur M. Sackler Museum, Gift of John Goelet, 1958.220; photo by Katya Kallsen © President and Fellows of Harvard College: 27

Courtesy Harvard Art Museum, Arthur M. Sackler Museum, Sarah C. Sears Collection, 1936.24; photo by Katya Kallsen © President and Fellows of Harvard College: 37

Courtesy and © the Lahore Museum, Lahore, Pakistan: 68, 75, 205, 229

Richard Shepard: 24–25, 42–45, 48–49, 56–57, 59 top, 128 top, 132–133, 144, 202, 204, 232, 242, 246–247, 248–249, 252

Samina Quraeshi & Richard Shepard: 32–33, 102–103, 108–109, 120, 122, 138, 139 top, 142, 276–277

Hafeez Mir: 22–23, 30–31, 34–35, 66–67, 87, 126, 136–137, 139 bottom, 143, 188, 209, 210–211, 212–213, 214–215

Kamil Khan Mumtaz: 46–47, 50–51, 52–53, 54–55, 58–59 bottom, 60–61, 266–267

Shireen Pasha: 118–119

Farooq Beg: 121

Calligraphy

Ghulam Murtaza: 63, 187

Ustad Gauhar Qalam: 15, 17, 19, 39, 77, 99, 200, 239, 263

Irfan Qureshi: i, 124, 223

Khurshid Raqam: 147, 165, 241

Lahore: Data Ganj Bakhsh Hujwiri

Lahore: Mian Mir

Lahore: Madho Lal Husain

Kasur: Bulleh Shah

Multan: Shaikh Rukn-i-Alam

Delhi: Nizamuddin Auliya

Ajmer: Khwaja Muinuddin Hasan Chishti

Bhit Shah: Shah Abdul Latif